MISS POPPY'S GUIDE

TO RAISING

PERFECTLY HAPPY CHILDREN

MISS POPPY'S GUIDE TO RAISING PERFECTLY HAPPY CHILDREN

ELAINE ADDISON

ILLUSTRATIONS BY SAM HOLLAND

Collins

First published in 2005 by Collins
An imprint of **HarperCollins** *Publishers*
77-85 Fulham Palace Road
Hammersmith
London W6 8JB

The Collins website address is **www.collins.co.uk**

Collins is a registered trademark of HarperCollins Publishers Ltd

11	10	09	08	07	06	05
7	6	5	4	3	2	1

Text © Elaine Addison 2005
Illustrations © Sam Holland 2005

Miss Poppy's Guide to Raising Perfectly Happy Children

First US edition 2005

HarperCollins books may be purchased for educational, business, or sales
promotional use. For information please write: Special Markets Department,
HarperCollins Publishers Inc., 10 East 53rd Street, New York, NY 10022.

EDITOR: Adam Parfitt
DESIGN: Valerie Fong
ILLUSTRATIONS: Sam Holland

A catalogue record for this book is available from the British Library

ISBN - 10: 0-06-082826-9
ISBN - 13: 978-0-06082826-4

Colour Reproduction, Printed and Bound by Butler & Tanner Ltd, Frome

CONTENTS

MISS POPPY'S ESSENTIAL INGREDIENTS
FOR RAISING HAPPY CHILDREN

'Children are likely to live up to what you believe of them.'
— LADY BIRD JOHNSON

Heaps of common sense
An abundance of energy
Pocketfuls of patience
A sense of humour
The ability to be tastefully tactful and devilishly devious
Imagination

Monday's child is fair of face
Tuesday's child is full of grace
Wednesday's child is full of woe
Thursday's child has far to go
Friday's child is loving and giving
Saturday's child works hard for a living
And the child that is born on the Sabbath day
Is bonny and blithe, and good and gay

As I think back eighteen years ago to the start of my nannying career, I recall a fresh-faced, bubbly, vivacious girl dressed impeccably in her navy uniform, straw boater and sensible flat shoes. As I wandered the paths of Hampstead Heath in London and Central Park in New York City with my charges, I was always being stopped by overexcited Japanese tourists to pose for pictures in the hope that I was 'Merry Pippins'! I was full to the brim with idealism and romantic notions of raising perfectly polite children quite easily. I had a rather old-fashioned yet sensibly written folder of practical and theoretical information about childcare, a natural affinity towards children and an enthusiastic curiosity about almost everything. These, I assumed, would be enough as I began my career all those years ago.

An older, wiser version of that idealistic nanny looks back in astonishment at how much there was to learn and discover about children and childcare in general. I have gained an enormous amount of practical, hands-on experience working for families with as many as four children under my sole charge. Sometimes I have worked closely and happily with the mother or father sharing in the care of two or three children. Occasionally I have worked with other nannies or had the assistance of an au pair to help lessen the load of looking after several children. I have bravely stepped into households where many other nannies (thirty-eight, to be precise) have fled in horror. I have worked with children from different countries and cultures; I have worked in great mansions and castles as well as council houses and suburban semis. My real-life experiences are vast and diverse; from them I have gained a wealth of information, insight and knowledge about children and their needs. I would like to share this with you.

During my travels I have had the privilege and honour of playing a part in many different childhoods – some for just for a few weeks or months at a time, others for several years. My memories of each and every child are still so vivid: the joy, curiosity and excitement of a new beginning, and then the long, sad farewells when it is time to move on to my next charge. I still see many of my charges today, and have had the pleasure of watching and admiring as they grow into kind, thoughtful and interesting young adults. It always astounds me how fast it all goes, but what is most interesting to me is what my charges remember about the time I have spent with them. It's always the same things: the sweet little sayings last thing at night before going to sleep; getting wrapped in a fluffy towel after bath time and being unravelled like a Swiss roll; nursery tea parties galore; picnics inside and out; clean-up games; creating obstacle courses inside on rainy days; baking Christmas cookies to give to their teachers. Children remember all the little extras that make the rituals of their daily life much more fun and appealing.

My recipe for good childcare is simple: provide the safety and security of a familiar routine; set clear limits and boundaries in order to make them feel loved and cared for and to teach respect; but most importantly, make it fun and play together. Sprinkle an element of fun whenever you can and teach through play as often as possible. It will improve your spirits as much as theirs.

All of my charges have shared in the delight of getting to know Miss Poppy, a persona I invented many years ago. Miss Poppy has learned to deal with all kinds of issues such as not wanting to go to bed, disgusting table manners and not wanting to eat, general rudeness and disrespect, potty-training and tantrums. Whatever particular stage my charge is going through, I invent a Miss Poppy story with a main character strongly resembling my charge so they can relate to him or her. I create a series of adventures closely resembling my charge's latest activities and fun-loving ways and games, and then introduce these games into their daily routine to great excitement and sound results. Miss Poppy has become a fantastic vehicle through which to execute my philosophy by turning everyday stages and chores into something personal, special and most of all fun.

Every household I have entered has been different. As a professional nanny, my job has as much to do with observation, learning and understanding as it does teaching, caring and nurturing. All families have their own individual style and dynamic. Their children assimilate, fit in and grow into becoming a part of that family unit. This is why I believe it is essential for you to develop your own individual, unique routine and way of doing things. Take what you can from my knowledge and experience as Miss Poppy, and follow her guidelines, but adapt all this to you, your lifestyle and your children in general. My experience has taught me that each child develops differently, but they all eventually get to where they are going.

I have chosen to begin this book at the age of six months, as I believe from my experience that this is a time when children really begin to travel through their different and challenging stages as they leave babyhood behind. Often it is a time when mothers or fathers return back to work and the child experiences day care, a child minder or a nanny for the first time. I hope that with the help of Miss Poppy, these transitional times can be made smoother for all of you.

I have yet to meet a child who does not respond to play and laughter, whatever language, learning or social barriers there are. Remember this in times of need or distress: children are children and they need as much fun and laughter in their lives as they do firm guidance, regular routines and clear limits and boundaries. Pop a sprinkling of each into a bowl, mix it all up and there you have it: Miss Poppy's guide to raising perfectly happy children.

CHAPTER ONE:

6 months – 1 year

'There isn't any formula or method.
You learn to love by loving – by paying attention and doing what
one thereby discovers has to be done.' – ALDOUS HUXLEY

'Sprinkle joy.' – RALPH WALDO EMERSON

Babies of any age are adorable, but at six months they really start
to come into their own with their cute little Buddha-shaped
bodies and those perfectly kissable rosy cheeks. I love this stage:
every day brings something new and exciting for both of you to
learn and discover about each other.

The advances they make during this period are astounding: their
babbling sounds will soon become first words, their physical
movements lead to first steps, their first taste of solid foods, their
first teeth. They start to develop preferences and attachments, and
their likes and dislikes become quite apparent. It is fascinating to
watch their personality begin to develop and shine through. Their
characters are being formed; they should be gently nurtured, their
curiosity encouraged. And so it begins, the great adventure. In the
words of Dr Seuss: 'Oh! the places you'll go …'

In this chapter we will discuss that amazing time between six
months and one year. We will start by looking at the business of
weaning and feeding your child – a subject that I have noticed
often causes parents a certain amount of worry. We will then look
at the importance of establishing a daily routine that works for
both you and your baby, and how that daily routine will help you
to encourage the one thing that I know all parents dream about –
a good night's sleep! Following that, I will explain the ways in
which you can expect your baby to grow physically, and how you
can encourage them to increase their mobility by making sure
that everything around them is perfectly safe. Life with a baby is

of course not always a bed of roses. We shall be looking at what causes the baby blues and what you can do to counteract them. Finally I shall give you a few ideas about how working parents can make sure they start learning how to juggle their new responsibilities, and how you can ensure that your baby will have plenty of the one commodity that is most important to them at this – or indeed any – age: fun!

BABY BISTRO

'Man is born to eat.' – ANONYMOUS

> *Pease pudding hot*
> *Pease pudding cold*
> *Pease pudding in the pot*
> *Nine days old*
> *Some like it hot*
> *Some like it cold*
> *Some like it in the pot*
> *Nine days old*

Weaning your baby on to solid food normally starts somewhere around six months. I find it usually depends on their size: if they weighed in at nine pounds or above at birth, they tend to start to need food sooner; others can wait – it really depends on the baby. The important thing to remember is not to panic if your child is still only downing pints of milk while your neighbour's baby of the same age seems to have developed a taste for gourmet delicacies. They all seem to catch up with each other in the course of the first year.

Start weaning around six months

If you have been breastfeeding, by the time your child is six months old you may have given some thought to weaning your baby off the breast, if you have not begun to do so already. The important thing to remember is to do it gradually, both for your sake and the baby's. Your child needs to be introduced to the bottle gradually, and you need to ensure that your milk production is reduced in stages so that you do not suffer engorgement which can be very painful and lead to infection.

Food is a difficult thing for your baby to master. It's good to take your time and slowly introduce simple, fresh organic foods. Weaning happens gradually over the course of a few months, and will not affect their daily intake of breast or formula milk. This should continue as normal because the small amount of foods you will be offering will not contain sufficient amounts of the essential proteins, fats, carbohydrates, vitamins and minerals that your baby needs to grow. The milk still provides this, and will only be replaced as the main source of nutrients around the age of twelve to fourteen months.

For the first week of weaning, choose a meal time when your baby is in good humour and moderately hungry – overtired or over-hungry babies get very upset if you remove their milk source, even for a second, and we want this to be a pleasant experience – and begin by offering breast milk or a bottle of formula milk. If your baby is able to sit up, put them into their high chair, with cushions if need be to prop them up. If they are not yet sitting up, you may have to hold them on your lap, or put them in a car seat. Place a little cotton bib loosely around them. Mix up a small amount – one or two teaspoons – of organic baby rice with a spot of their milk. Serve it to them on a plastic baby spoon rather than a metal one which they might find a bit harsh at first, and gently position it in their mouth and watch the wonderful faces you'll be rewarded with. I think the first look is of pure astonishment, as they don't quite know what to make of it.

Make sure your baby is not overtired or overhungry

If they refuse the spoon at first, dip your little finger in the rice and offer them a taste. Take your time and be prepared to sit and wait a while as they discover the texture and taste and pull many a funny face. Often they stick their tongue out or open their mouths as if to say, 'More, please!' Don't be tempted to pile it in – just a couple of teaspoons a day is enough at first. Finish off by offering them the rest of the bottle of formula milk or more breast milk, and continue to feed them for the rest of the day with their scheduled daily milk feeds.

Some babies take to solid foods like a duck to water; others just take their time, having a little taste here and there but generally preferring their milk. Do not worry about this: they all grow up with healthy appetites in the end. If they don't instantly take to their first helping of baby rice, leave it for a day or two and then try again. Once they have accepted it for about a week, you can gradually introduce a purée of fruit. Bananas, stewed apples or stewed pears are always a good bet at first. It is a good idea not to give mixtures of fruits (or vegetables) in the first few weeks – now is a good time to see if there are any foods that your little one does not tolerate well; if foods are mixed together, you may not be able to identify which one is problematic. Begin by mixing the purée with a couple of teaspoons of organic baby rice cereal, and serve it to them just as you did the week before, always offering the milk first, then the solids, and finishing up with the milk. By the end of the second week you can offer the fruit all by itself, and you should see it go down very smoothly indeed. Continue to feed them their regular milk feeds as usual.

Don't be alarmed by funny-coloured dirty nappies. Remember that their digestive systems are just beginning to function fully, and from now on I'm afraid the nappies are only going to get worse!

The next week you can try vegetables – perhaps a purée of carrot, swede or sweet potato. Repeat the same procedure at the beginning of the week by mixing in a couple of teaspoons of organic baby rice cereal with the purée. By the end of the week try the vegetable purée alone. (Remember always to begin and end with breast or formula milk and to continue to feed them their regular milk feeds as usual.)

Continue the regular milk feed

By the end of the first month of weaning, your baby can begin to eat two meals a day. This does not affect their regular milk feed which should still continue as usual. They are usually starving in the mornings, so give them their milk first and then a breakfast of two teaspoons of fruit purée. You can always use baby rice to bulk out a fruit purée if it seems necessary. If the consistency is too thick, add a drop of their milk to make it smoother. Finish with milk or, if they have drunk it all, try introducing a drink of water from a feeding cup with a sucking spout. For lunch, offer two teaspoons of vegetable purée followed by breast or bottled milk. Then continue to feed breast milk or formula milk as usual.

> By offering them a feeding cup from an early age, you are encouraging independence and giving them time to practise the art of self-feeding. Drinking cups come in a variety of shapes and sizes, and some are leak-free, so if your child holds them upside down or hurls them across the room, the liquid

will stay inside. The fact that they have a sucking spout rather than a teat means that your baby will have to work a bit harder to get the liquid flowing, but they will soon get the hang of it. Learning to drink from a cup can be a messy business, so do have a bib handy. You could also give them a cup of water in the bath, where they can make as much mess as they like – and have fun too!

By the second month they will be ready to expand their palate slightly and add protein in the form of chicken, meat or lentils. Chicken and fish can be poached until tender and then puréed *Broaden the* with a spot of the cooking water or a little milk, then mashed *choice in the* together with a vegetable of choice for a delicious casserole flavour. *second month* Gradually your baby can start to eat three meals a day. At this stage, you can drop one milk feed if it seems necessary, but you should ensure that the actual amount of milk they drink throughout the day remains the same – about 550 ml (1 pint).

SAFETY TIP:

Never leave a baby unattended during feeding, as choking can occur. If you suspect your baby is choking, lift both their arms up in the air to open the airways. If they are unable to cough it up, place them upside down, face down on your lap and give them a good pat on the upper back, between the shoulders. Repeat if the food is still stuck. Always call for medical assistance if your baby stops breathing. Cuddle, comfort and reassure afterwards.

WHAT YOUR BABY CAN AND CAN'T EAT

There are certain foods that you should not give your child below certain ages; and there are foods that I tend to avoid giving children until they reach a certain age – not because they are harmful, but because they can be a little strong for their sensitive palates. Below is a simple list of dos and don'ts for you to follow, but remember: just because a baby can eat a certain food, it doesn't mean that they will. I have known children who devour courgettes (zucchini) at the age of seven months, and others who won't touch them until they are a year old – or older!

Foods to avoid because they can be harmful

Salt. You should not give your baby any salt, as their kidneys cannot process it. Use in moderation only after one year.

Sugar. This can be very harmful to growing teeth.

Honey. This can contain a dangerous bacteria which your child cannot cope with until they are one.

Nuts and seeds. Small children can easily choke on these, and if given at an early age they can increase the likelihood of a nut allergy. It's best to wait until four-five years old, although smooth peanut butter may be given after one year if your family has no history of peanut allergy.

Gluten. All wheat-, rye- and barley-based products, such as certain breakfast cereals, flour, bread and rusks, must be avoided if your family has a history of gluten intolerance.

Eggs. Babies can be severely allergic to egg whites. Well-cooked egg yolks can be given at seven months but wait until nine months to serve a well-cooked whole egg.

Shellfish. White boneless fish can be given at seven months and oily fish at nine months. Shellfish, however, should be avoided for the first three years as it may cause allergies.

Citrus fruits. These are too severe for a very young child's digestive system so wait until your baby is eight-nine months. This includes citrus juice, which should then be served diluted (one part juice to four parts boiled water).

Soft and unpasteurised cheeses. These can contain bacteria which can be very harmful to babies. Avoid for the first three years.

Low-fat milk products. Cutting back on fat is a good idea for adults, but not for small children, especially those under the age of two.

6 months

Good first foods

Puréed fruits and vegetables

Purées of meat and poultry

Full-fat milk products. These include yogurt and fromage frais.
Cow's milk may be used in cooking, but should not replace breast
or formula milk until your baby is one year old. Remember to
continue their regular milk feeds.

TYPICAL DAILY MENU

Breakfast

Creamed organic baby rice with mashed banana

Lunch

Purée of fresh carrot

7 months

During this time, you should gradually start to introduce foods
that are lumpier in texture, and finger foods that your baby
can try and eat by themselves. Your child needs to learn how
to chew, and the longer you leave this, the more difficult it will
be. Learning to chew also encourages the development of the
muscles needed for speech.

Good foods to introduce now

Wheat-based foods and cereals, including brown bread, pasta, oats,
brown rice and low-sugar breakfast cereals

Fresh, boneless fish

Fruits such as peaches, mango, plums and heavily diluted juices such
as apple and peach (one part juice to four parts water)

TYPICAL DAILY MENU

Breakfast
Breast milk or formula milk
Purée of pear mixed with 2 teaspoons organic baby rice

Mid-morning snack
Breast milk or formula milk

Lunch
2–4 teaspoons mashed chicken with a purée of vegetable
2 teaspoons fruit purée
A beaker of fresh water. If milk is demanded then supply it;
   if not save it for the afternoon

Mid-afternoon snack
Breast milk or formula milk

Tea
2–4 teaspoons puréed vegetable
Breast milk or formula milk

Supper
Breast milk or formula milk

A balanced diet
Once solid foods are an established part of the daily diet, at about
7 months, try to give your baby the following each day:
Two or three servings of carbohydrate, such as potatoes, rice,
bread or pasta
Two or three servings of fresh fruit and vegetables, either as
finger foods or as part of the meal
One serving of protein, such as poultry, fish or lentils

8–10 months

As your child becomes more confident with food, try to introduce a new food at least once every week. As your baby's teeth cut through, you can offer a slightly lumpier texture of food. Your baby can also begin learning how to feed themselves if you give them their very own plastic spoon. Most of it will end up on them or the floor rather than in their mouth, so keep a spoon of your own handy, and sneak one or two spoonfuls in when you can. But don't discourage them, or be deterred by the mess: this is only the beginning. If you are worried about mess, put a plastic tablecloth under the high chair, and use one of those plastic bibs with a curved trough at the bottom to catch any spillage. And of course your baby has to squash all the collected mush – great fun indeed!

Try out one new food a week

TYPICAL DAILY MENU

Breakfast

Baby rice or porridge mixed with breast milk or formula milk

Half a ripe banana, held in the hand

2 small soldiers of toast made from brown bread and buttered very slightly with unsalted butter

Breast milk, or formula milk served in a cup (if a fuss is created, use a bottle)

Mid-morning snack

Breast milk or formula milk

Lunch

Flakes of white fish (poached and de-boned), mashed potato and florets of soft broccoli

Slices of fresh, ripe mango

A cup of fresh water

Mid-afternoon snack
Breast milk or formula milk

Tea
Mashed avocado with cottage cheese and slices of peeled cucumber
An organic fruit-flavoured yogurt
A cup of fresh water

Supper
Breast milk or formula milk

10–12 months

Between ten and twelve months your baby will be ready for a wide selection of finger foods such as slices of cheese, blanched carrot sticks or chunks of watermelon.

Try finger foods now

TYPICAL DAILY MENU

Breakfast
Scrambled eggs with soldiers of toast made from brown bread and
    buttered very slightly with unsalted butter
Skinned, sliced peaches
Breast milk, or formula milk served in a cup (if a fuss is created,
    use a bottle)

Mid-morning snack

Peeled apple slices

Breast milk, or formula milk served in a cup (if a fuss is created, use a bottle)

Lunch

Meatballs made of finely minced pure beef, pasta twirls and grated cheese

Melon slices

A cup of fresh water

Mid-afternoon snack

Sliced kiwi fruit

Breast milk, or formula milk served in a cup (if a fuss is created, use a bottle)

Tea

Mashed lentils with spinach and cubes of tofu

A small fromage frais

A cup of fresh water

Supper

Breast milk or formula milk

RECIPES FROM MISS POPPY'S PANTRY

I believe we are what we eat, and an early introduction to healthy, nutritious food is one of the best things you can do for your baby. Start your baby with the kind of food you intend them to eat later on in their life.

Basic nutrition is quite simple to master. Think fresh, local, seasonal vegetables and fruits – organic if possible. They provide lots of vitamins, minerals and roughage. Free-range chicken and eggs, organic meats, fresh fish, lentils, beans and other pulses provide much-needed protein. Dairy products such as pasteurised cottage cheese and hard cheese, yogurt and cow's milk add to their protein consumption. Mix in a nice helping of complex carbohydrates such as potatoes, brown and wholemeal breads and pastas of all shapes and sizes. Don't forget brown or white rice, oats, semolina and other cereals and grains. Your goal is to serve a varied selection of each of these foods daily, to create a perfectly well-balanced diet that will keep them fit and healthy.

When introducing a new food into your baby's diet, be careful to observe any reactions that may appear out of the ordinary: itchy, swollen eyes, skin rashes, wheezy chests or runny noses are all signs of food allergies. If you are at all worried, remove the culprit food from the baby's diet immediately and consult your local GP who will offer help and advice. People can develop intolerances to any type of food, but the most common are dairy products, nuts and seeds (particularly peanuts), fruits and wheat products (including flour). The following recipes all state what ages they are suitable for.

This is based on whether the recipe contains anything that is actually harmful to your child. However, babies take to different foods at different ages, and if you wean your child later than six months, you may find that they are not ready to accept certain foods just yet. Give it time, and be patient. If they don't take to a particular food or recipe, offer them something you know they like and try again a few days, or weeks, later.

VEGETABLE AND FRUIT PURÉES (6 MONTHS AND UP)

Cooking one carrot and a single green bean always seems a bit silly to me, so I tend to make a whole batch of, for example, fresh carrot. Simply boil them till tender, purée into a pulp and pop them into an ice-cube tray or old yogurt pots. You can then freeze them for future use. You can do the same thing with most vegetables and fruits so that you have a handy selection from which to pick and choose.

BAKED SWEET POTATO MASH (6 MONTHS AND UP)

1 medium sweet potato

Pre-heat the oven to 220°C/425°F/Gas Mark 7. Wash and dry the sweet potato, then wrap it in tin foil. Place in the oven and cook for about an hour until the flesh feels soft when pronged with a skewer. Cut the potato in half, scrape out all the tender orange centre, and mash with a fork until nice and fluffy.

MANGO FROMAGE FRAIS (6 MONTHS AND UP)

1 ripe mango
1 dessertspoon natural fromage frais

Peel the mango and slice wedges of the fruit from the pit. Mash with a fork, mix into the fromage frais and serve.

APPLE AND OAT DELIGHT (6 MONTHS AND UP)

1 apple
1 dessertspoon whole oats
full-fat cow's milk, or formula milk

Peel, core and chop the apple. Place in a pan with 1 tablespoon water, cover with a lid and boil for 3–4 minutes until the apple is tender. Purée in a blender, or mash with a fork. Place the oats in a pan with twice the volume of milk, bring to the boil and then simmer, stirring constantly, until soft and gooey. Add the purée of apple, cool and serve.

CLASSIC FISH PIE (7 MONTHS AND UP)

1 medium potato
1 carrot
a handful of spinach
full-fat cow's milk
50g (2oz) fresh boneless fillet of white fish such as cod or plaice
Cheddar cheese, grated

Peel and chop the potato and carrot. Wash the spinach thoroughly. Place the potato in boiling water and boil for 15 minutes. Add the carrot and boil for another 5 minutes. Finally add the spinach and boil for another 3 minutes. Drain and blend with a splash of milk until smooth.

Place the fish in a small pan, add a little milk and poach for a few minutes until tender. Flake the fish, check for bones and then blend it into the mash. Sprinkle with a little grated cheese and serve.

BUTTERNUT SQUASH BABY RISOTTO (7 MONTHS AND UP)

1 medium butternut squash, peeled and cut into small pieces
a handful of Arborio risotto rice, washed

Place the squash in a pan of boiling water and boil for 10 minutes. Remove the squash with a slotted spoon and save the boiling water. Place the cooked squash and the rice in a separate pan and add a little of the boiling water. Cook on a gentle heat, stirring continuously, until the water has been absorbed, then add a little more. Continue this for about 20 minutes until the rice has softened to a rich, creamy texture. Mash the risotto together with a fork, cool and serve.

SPINACH AND RED LENTIL SURPRISE (8 MONTHS AND UP)

75g (3oz) red lentils
a handful of spinach leaves
1 tablespoon pasteurised cottage cheese

Wash the lentils well, picking out any small stones. Place in twice the volume of boiling water and cook until soft, about 35 minutes, adding more water if needed. Wash the spinach leaves well, removing hard stalks, and add to the lentils during the last 3-4 minutes of cooking, covering with a tight-fitting lid. Drain the liquid and set aside a small amount for blending. Purée the lentils and spinach in a blender along with a small amount of cooking liquid. Stir in a dollop of cottage cheese and serve.

BUBBLE AND SQUEAK (8 MONTHS AND UP)

1 large potato
a small stem of broccoli
a handful of peas
full-fat cow's milk
a dollop of pasteurised cottage cheese

Peel and chop the potato and place in a pan of boiling water for 15 minutes. Remove the pan from the heat. Chop the florets of broccoli from the stem and add them along with the peas to the boiling water. Boil for another 7–10 minutes until everything is tender. Drain all the water, add a spot of full-fat cow's milk and a dollop of cottage cheese, and mash together.

CLASSIC COTTAGE PIE (8 MONTHS AND UP)

1 medium potato
1 carrot
½ a small swede
full-fat cow's milk
50g (2oz) minced beef or lamb
sunflower oil for frying
Cheddar cheese, grated

Peel the potato, carrot and swede and cut them all into small pieces. Place the potato and swede in a pan of boiling water and cook for 20 minutes. Add the chopped carrot and cook for about

another 5 minutes until everything is tender. Drain, add a splash of milk and mash together.

Fry your meat in a tiny drop of sunflower oil until golden brown. Place the meat in a small bowl or ramekin and top with the mash. Sprinkle with a little grated cheese and serve.

EGGCELLENT SCRAMBLED EGGS (9 MONTHS AND UP)

1 egg
full-fat cow's milk
a little butter
1 tablespoon pasteurised cottage cheese

Whisk the egg along with a drop of milk. Heat a little butter in a pan, add the egg and stir continuously until well cooked. Remove from the heat and stir in a dollop of cottage cheese.

FISHY RICE JAMBOREE (9 MONTHS AND UP)

a handful of white or brown rice, washed
50g (2oz) fresh boneless fillet of white fish such as cod or plaice
full-fat cow's milk
1 green or yellow courgette (zucchini)
a little sunflower oil for frying
1 hard-boiled egg

Boil the rice in twice the volume of water for 10–12 minutes if using white rice, or 15–20 minutes if using brown. Place the fish in a small pan, add a little milk and poach for a few minutes until tender. Remove the fish from the milk and set aside. Chop the courgette into small pieces and fry in a tiny amount of sunflower oil until soft and golden. Chop the hard-boiled egg into small pieces. Flake the fish into small pieces, check for bones, then add to the rice along with the courgette and the egg. Stir and serve.

TEETHING AND ILLNESS

Your baby will begin to develop teeth any time from six months onwards – if they have not done so already. The first little white bumps to appear are the incisors at the bottom front, followed by those at the upper front about two months later. By twelve months your baby could have up to a dozen teeth, but they may have to wait another year and a half for a complete set of gnashers.

It's best not to make too much of a fuss about teething, as it's going to be a constant part of their life for the next two years. It will cause grouchiness and inevitable sleepless nights at times. You might notice that your baby is a little out of sorts, not their usual bubbly self. They may also be dribbling and drooling all over the place. As time goes on you will learn to recognise the other classic signs of teething: slight fevers, despicably dirty nappies, a loss of appetite due to swollen gums. All you can do is be patient and offer them comfort. Keep several soft, clean cotton mini-bibs (which are shorter and less bulky than regular bibs) to catch any dribble and drool and keep them comfy and dry. I tend not to use the antiseptic, numbing teething gels they sell at chemists. I prefer the old-fashioned remedy of a spot of clove oil diluted down with safflower oil. Rub it on their swollen gums for slight relief. One can also offer great comfort in the form of cold, hard foods such as a chilled carrot stick or piece of apple, to chew and suck on. The coldness numbs the sore gums temporarily, and eases the pain.

TEETHING TAMERS

Icy cold carrot and celery sticks

A whole, chilled peeled apple (lots of fun to hold and drop on the floor)

A gel teething toy, frozen first in the fridge

A clean, cold, damp face cloth straight from the fridge

Hard teething biscuits
Crusts of bread, served chilled
Your finger, served chilled
A cold drink of water or diluted fruit juice
A cold yogurt or chilled puree of fruit

The dirty nappies that often come hand in hand with teething can lead to terribly sore nappy rash. Make sure you change their nappies as often as you can. When you do so, ensure that they are scrupulously clean and dry, and apply plenty of nappy-rash cream. If your child is prone to diarrhoea when they are teething, ensure that they drink plenty of fluids to replace what they are losing.

Teething often goes hand in hand with weaning the baby off the breast. When this happens, you stop sharing your antibodies with the baby, and they become more susceptible to illness. It's possible that you will find that your baby has been perfectly healthy all the time you have been breastfeeding them, and as soon as you stop they suffer an endless stream of colds and other illnesses. This is perfectly normal, and should only be a cause for concern if the illness is still there after a few days, or seems to be getting progressively worse. For more information on what to do if your child is unwell, see pages 110-116.

DAYTIME ROUTINE

'Ritual is like play: it requires something of the childlike.'
— GERTRUD MUELLER NELSON

By the age of three or four months, you will probably have noticed a regular pattern to your baby's behaviour: they will wake at certain times, for example, or be more alert or sleepy at certain times. Soon they will start to have regular feeding times. Bottle-fed babies tend to fall into a feeding routine more easily than breastfed babies. This is because formula milk is harder to digest than breast milk, so breastfed babies get hungry more quickly.

When they reach the age of six months, a more definite routine will have manifested itself in some way: they will generally be waking up at the same time each day, and even if you are feeding 'on demand', they will have established a pattern of eating more or less at the same time. Now is the time to start to develop a more concrete daily routine so that you can impose some sort of structure on your day. It will allow you to feel more in control, and your baby will feel more secure. Children derive great comfort, happiness and security by simple things such as knowing when it's time to eat, time to go to sleep and time to play – all the basic daily activities which enable them to thrive and grow. A good daily routine will teach your baby the order of daily life, and will establish good eating habits and good sleeping patterns, both of which will lead to good learning and social skills in the future. Some people dismiss routines as being unnecessarily stringent, but my experience has taught me that they are the foundation of everything.

This is not to say that you cannot be flexible; of course you can – indeed you need to be in today's frenetic way of living. Your baby must fit into your lifestyle and the way you live. A basic routine,

Establish a routine by six months

however, is not that hard to sustain, and you will find that the best way to find a routine that will serve the needs of both you and your baby – as well as the rest of your family – is to let it happen organically. It is important not to expect too much at first – most routines take weeks to develop. Be encouraged by a ten-minute nap at a regular time each day, or by one meal at the appropriate time. My life revolves solely around babies and children, so I can devote my entire day to the care and well-being of my charges. I understand, however, how difficult it is for parents who have to raise children while holding down a demanding full-time job. So it's important that you take what you can from Miss Poppy's experience and knowledge in creating routines and schedules, and fit and adapt it into your own lifestyle. And don't despair if the prospect of establishing a routine around a hectic lifestyle seems impossibly daunting. Routines can be adapted to fit around almost any way of life, as I found out when I was asked to look after a little boy who had done more travelling in his first six months than most of us do in our entire lifetime …

FULLY TRAINED, EXPERIENCED BRITISH NANNY REQUIRED FOR HRH PRINCE OMAR (SEVEN MONTHS). LUXURIOUS HOMES, FLOATING PALACES, JET-SET LIFESTYLE IN DUBAI, LONDON, PARIS, ST TROPEZ AND NEW YORK CITY. MUST BE FLEXIBLE.

Omar was a delightful little sheikh who, before my arrival, had been fed and cared for by an entire harem of doting admirers. His entourage included several personal bodyguards, a personal chef and an entire army of domestic helpers – one to dress him, one to wash his clothes, one to fan him to sleep, one to fan him awake... This hotchpotch selection of carers jumped every time he murmured, and reacted mostly with food. He was constantly carried around, and never got the chance to learn how to move or crawl. As a result, the poor child was rounder than round. The important thing to remember, though, is that he was greatly loved and showered with affection. His carers weren't exactly doing anything wrong; rather they were doing too much of everything, which I have observed to have the same effect as doing too little. It is stifling and leads to insecurities and anxieties in their future lives.

Prince Omar had a lot of problems sleeping; as a result he tended to be grouchy a lot of the time and never really settled; this was accentuated by the fact that he was completely overstimulated and overfed. His day was always disrupted because of the amount of travelling and movement in his day-to-day life. His parents came from a nomadic tribe who had struck oil. Their natural instinct was to move all the time, but instead of tents in the desert, they preferred palatial mansions in cosmopolitan cities, and luxurious yachts floating around the Mediterranean. They moved wherever and whenever the whim took them, and we would generally get absolutely no warning.

Poor Prince Omar never knew whether he was coming or going, so it was time for me to put on my thinking cap and devise a plan of action simple enough for everyone to follow. The first thing was to develop a schedule of proper eating times: breakfast at seven o'clock, lunch at midday (or earlier if he seemed sleepy), tea at five o'clock and a bottle of milk at seven o'clock before bed. Meal times were to be kept calm – not too many people or distractions, in fact mostly just one on one at first so we could both concentrate.

Naps were introduced twice daily: one in the morning from nine until ten or half past (depending on how he had slept the previous night), and one after lunch at half past twelve until about two o'clock (or a bit later, depending on how long he had slept in the morning). I always managed to find a quiet spot, be it his buggy, the aeroplane seat or the back of a limo. It was difficult to get him to nap at first because his sleeping patterns had become quite irregular. I used his musical teddy bear to help him recognise when it was time to go to sleep, and everywhere we went I took his familiar soft blanket that smelled like home. With patience and persistence his routine began to take shape and the naps became easier and more established. He learned to fall asleep absolutely anywhere, bless him!

What I was able to offer Prince Omar was a simple, orderly routine that could be adapted to fit into his nomadic lifestyle. I met him years later, quite by chance. He was the size of a sumo wrestler and nearly crushed several of my ribs when he gave me a hug, but he nevertheless seemed happy and sweet-natured – oh, and completely overindulged (as all sheikhs should be!)

By the time your baby is six months old, you will have established some sort of pattern, whether you are feeding on demand or on a strictly four-hourly basis. Now, though, your baby will be staying awake for longer periods throughout the day, and demanding much more of your constant attention. Of course you will want to be with them during this time, helping them play, laugh, learn and discover; but it would be nice occasionally to make a grown-up telephone conversation without your little one chewing on the cord. This is when a routine comes into its own for both of you: you can get on with the things you have to do while your baby enjoys their

much-needed nap. Get it right and you can rely on having one or two hours of uninterrupted time during the day to play catch-up.

Depending on when your baby wakes up, set an official time to eat breakfast together – let's say seven o'clock. If your baby wakes earlier, try to encourage them to stay in their cot for a while by popping a couple of soft fabric books or a favourite toy in their cot – a little peace and quiet in the morning is not a bad way to start the day. Try not to rush in as soon as they wake up, but listen in on a baby monitor or by ear and wait for a moment to see if the initial crying subsides – it often does if they find something to distract them. Sometimes, however, they are just so hungry that you will need to go in and give them some milk immediately. They will appreciate a nappy change at this point, but mostly they will just be so happy to see you – before the hunger mood kicks in.

After breakfast, it's time to play a little game or two. There are so many ways to make your baby feel loved and special, but the best thing in the world you can do at this age is to play with them. Silly, simple, bouncing-on-the-knees games, hide-and-seek games, dropping the ball, pushing the ball – anything that involves movement, noise and facial expressions. See Miss Poppy's Guide to Having Fun at the end of this chapter for a few all-time favourites.

By now the morning will be well and truly underway, and it is time for their first nap. You should try and make this no later than nine o'clock – you will find that that first burst of energy wanes quite quickly, so catch it when you can. You will soon learn to tell if they are tired: simple signs include rubbing their eyes, being a bit grumpy and laying their head to one side. Pop them into their cot and expect them to sleep for about an hour. If at first you don't succeed, try and try again. At the beginning they may kick up a fuss; try to ignore it unless it turns into hysterical crying. If it does, go into the room and, without picking them up, reach down and comfort them by gently stroking and soothing them. Then be brave and try again. It is important that you stick to your guns and be persistent, understanding yet firm. As the days go on and you establish your routine, it will become easier – I promise. If they have had a wakeful night, they may sleep for longer than an hour. If you have plans or need to be somewhere, calmly wake them up if they are still fast asleep by stroking their back and gently talking to them. Pick them up and enjoy a good cuddle – a precious time for the two of you to treasure. Offer them a drink of water because they are probably thirsty, and this will help to liven them up a bit.

Make the morning nap no later then nine o'clock

Now is a good time for a morning outing. Babies don't have to go far – a change of scenery and a spot of fresh air does them the world of good – so whether you are off to do the shopping or simply having a walk in the park or just around the block, they will be happy to be out and about. Don't forget to pack your nappy bag.

Lunch should be at twelve noon, or thereabouts; if they seem hungry bring it forward to half past eleven. Try not to linger past midday, even if they don't appear particularly hungry, as before you know it they will have gone beyond their afternoon-nap time. Once you reach two or three o'clock, it's easier to skip the nap, but you'll then find that by five o'clock they will be awfully grotty, tired and desperate for a snooze which will inevitably play havoc with your bedtime schedule. So straight after lunch, at about half past twelve, pop them down for their afternoon nap, which usually lasts for two hours.

Lunch no later than noon

Wake them up as before with a drink of water to refresh them. As the routine kicks in they will start automatically waking at certain times as their body pattern begins to fall into a rhythm. The

Afternoon nap at half past twelve

afternoon should include (weather permitting) another outing – a walk to the park or a visit to friend's house, perhaps.

Teatime. Shall we say five o'clock? I think that's as good a time as any, but I always leave room for a bit of flexibility. They will be famished from all their social activity, but try to keep teatime short and sweet – no longer than half an hour – as they get bored and are ready for bath time by this point.

Let's recap:

TEN STEPS TO A ROUTINE

1. Observe your baby's feeding and sleeping times closely and write them down. Note their most alert and awake periods and their most sleepy and grumpy periods.
2. Create a definite bedtime for which to aim every night – anywhere between 6:30 p.m. and 7:30 p.m.
3. Create a definite bathtime which should be part of your evening wind down routine, preferably one hour before bedtime.
4. Establish three meal times - breakfast, lunch and dinner - and aim to keep them the same each day.
5. Introduce two naps per day, at specific times. One mid-morning - 9:30-10:30 a.m. - and one after lunch at 12:30-2:30 p.m.
6. Book doctors' appointments, baby classes and social occasions at times when you know your baby is most likely to be alert and awake, and not during nap time.
7. Be patient. Establishing a routine takes time and commitment. Take it one week at a time.
8. Be flexible. Work your individual routine around you, your baby and your commitments.
9. Fresh air! Include a definite time for a daily outing.
10. Keep a daily diary to remind yourself how far you have come.

MISS POPPY'S SUGGESTED DAYTIME ROUTINE FOR 6–12 MONTH-OLDS

Remember, you should only use this as a guideline for creating your very own personal routine, one that will suit you, your family and your baby best.

6.30–7 a.m.: Wakey-wakey, rise and shine!
7–7.30 a.m.: Breakfast
9–10 a.m.: Morning nap
10.30 a.m.: Outing
12 p.m.: Lunch
12.30–2.30 p.m.: Afternoon nap
3 p.m.: Outing
5 p.m.: Teatime
6 p.m.: Bath time
6.30–7 p.m.: Start the night-time routine

NIGHT-TIME ROUTINE

*'There was never a child so lovely
but his mother was glad to get him asleep.'*
– RALPH WALDO EMERSON

*Sleep, baby, sleep
Thy father guards the sheep
Thy mother shakes the dreamland tree
And from it fall sweet dreams for thee
Sleep, baby, sleep*

Babies do not naturally sleep through the night; their sleeping patterns have to be nurtured and supported by you. That said, by the age of six months, your baby is capable of sleeping through the night for ten to twelve hours, exceptions made for sickness, teething, separation anxiety or time-zone changes. I believe that sleep is habit forming – the more you get, the more you want – and as your daily routine becomes more established with fixed eating and sleeping times, the more sleep you will get at night.

Create good sleeping habits

A comfortable bedtime routine is similarly important. You need to create a calming and relaxed environment for both you and your baby to wind down at the end of a busy day, and repeat it at the same time every evening. Begin with bath time.

> *Charlie, Charlie, in the tub*
> *Charlie, Charlie, pulled out the plug*
> *Oh my goodness, oh my soul*
> *There goes Charlie down the hole*

Bath at six o'clock

A good time for a bath is around six o'clock, straight after tea. You will find it helpful to prepare all the items you will need beforehand, and place them in the bathroom so there is never a need to leave the baby in the bath unattended.

MISS POPPY'S LIST OF BATH TIME ESSENTIALS

A clean nappy
Nappy cream
A nappy bin or disposable nappy sack
A night gown, babygro or pyjamas
A natural sponge or soft face cloth
A natural, non-perfumed soap or baby bath
A soft, fluffy towel
A baby hairbrush or comb
Bath toys

Run a moderately warm bath, so the water is up to their waist when sitting. If you prefer, you can use a special seat which sticks to the bottom of the tub with suction pads so you can keep your hands free. I like to give babies as much independence as possible so I plop them down sitting on top of a non-stick bath mat. I keep both of my arms over the tub at all times to catch any slippery babies. Pop in several bath toys to amuse them while you gently wash away the day's dirt and grime with a soft cloth or natural sponge. Hair-washing can be kept to a minimum; you only really need to rinse off any encrusted food with warm water. If you do use a baby shampoo, use very little and water it down – the detergents can sometimes play havoc with their delicate skin. To wash their hair, lean them back slightly and gently sponge water down the back of their scalp. If water does run into their eyes, don't panic, stay calm and quickly wipe it away – it's actually not a bad thing for them to get used to water on their face. I usually find that giving them a toy to play with makes them immediately forget about the water dripping on them.

MISS POPPY'S LIST OF BABY'S FIRST BATH TIME TOYS

Go for soft and squeaky with no sharp edges – all bath toys are immediately tasted!

A squeaky rubber duck

A plastic cup, bottle or empty container

A colourful face cloth

A rubber boat

A waterproof book

When it's time to get them out, simply lift them up and plop them on to a soft, fluffy towel and rub them dry. Now it's time for a quick brush of their tooth (or teeth) with warm water using a soft baby toothbrush. Be careful – babies can become quite captivated with a simple toothbrush, and they love to chew on them; but they are rather dangerous and should never be left with

an unsupervised baby. If they are a wriggler, give them something to hold and play with while you dress them in their nightclothes. It is a good idea to keep those toys for dressing purposes only so that they don't get bored of them. Now brush or comb their hair and you have a picture-perfect baby, almost ready for bed. As the wind-down time has begun, keep the mood calm and low-key as you have a last drink of milk and look at a book together (see Miss Poppy's Guide to Having Fun for a list of good books for children of this age). If your baby seems a little overexcited for bedtime, calm them down by gently massaging their back, shoulders, arms and legs. Babies loved to be touched – gentle stroking reassures them and makes them feel loved.

Most babies move around a lot during the night, kicking away their blankets and then waking up because they are cold, so I always introduce a baby sleeping bag at around three months of age. Baby sleeping bags are an all-in-one garment, usually made of soft padded cotton or flannel fabric. They resemble a sleeping bag at the bottom, and leave enough room for your baby to wriggle their legs around, but fit snugly like a pinafore at the top. You put them on top of their nightclothes, and there is a zip at the side or the front. Baby sleeping bags mean that there is no need for covers, and your child keeps warm all night long. Once they get old enough to stand up in the cot, I tend to switch to a sleep suit – like a baby sleeping bag only with legs at the bottom to stop them tripping up.

Make sure the room is not too hot or too cold – 16–21°C/62–70°F is recommended – draw the curtains and switch on the baby monitor. Place your baby in the cot so that their feet are almost touching the bottom end – that way you won't run the risk of them sliding down the cot and being smothered by their blankets, if you are using them. I like to place a musical mobile above the crib and use it to initiate sleep, so I simply wind it up and tuck them in. Say goodnight and then make a swift exit. Don't dawdle!

BEING SIDS SAFE

Sudden Infant Death Syndrome, or SIDS, is something that worries all new parents. Fortunately, a lot of research has been done, and there are some simple steps you can take to reduce the likelihood of this terrible phenomenon:

Choose a safe, comfortable, up-to-date cot (crib) with a firm, well-fitting mattress. The distance between the bars of the cot should be no more than 6.5cm (2½in)

Make sure the room is not too hot, and your baby is not overdressed. Overheating has been found to be a contributing factor to SIDS, so make sure the temperature of your baby's room is between 16-21°C/ 62-70°F. If your child feels hot, or is perspiring at the back of the neck, remove a layer of clothing

Lie your child on their back when you put them in the cot – this has been shown to reduce the risk of SIDS dramatically

Keep the cot free of decorative cot bunkers, pillows, soft toys and extra bedding, as these can cause overheating and suffocation

Babies subjected to second-hand cigarette smoke have shown an increased risk of SIDS

Star light, star bright
First star I see tonight
I wish I may, I wish I might
Have the wish I wish tonight

BEDTIME BLUES

'Childrearing myth number one: labour ends when the baby is born.'
— ANONYMOUS

If your baby refuses to go to sleep, there may be a simple reason such as hunger, a dirty nappy, illness, a noisy distraction or a change in time zone. I have heard every excuse in the book to explain why a baby won't go to sleep, from the inevitable 'We can't bear to be apart' – which is understandable in certain circumstances – to the bizarre 'He likes me to get into the cot with him' (she did, too, all six feet of her, squeezed in like Houdini!). Hunger and a change of nappy can be easily fixed, but with illness I'm afraid it's inevitable that their sleep and yours will be disturbed. As far as noise goes, I like to get my charges used to some sort of noise as early as possible, so I tend to leave a classical radio station on quite low. That way I am able to stomp about a bit without having to tiptoe past their bedroom door. Other noises should be kept to a minimum until they drop off to sleep.

It could of course be that they have not learned to put themselves to sleep yet. If you've covered all of the above and you know that your baby is clean, well fed and not ill, then let the teaching begin.

I know how tempting it is to rock, lull and stroke your beautiful baby to sleep, but by the age of six months they are capable of putting themselves to sleep; it is something they should learn at a young age, and it will make their early years much happier and more comfortable. You must get them used to their own cot (crib) as soon as possible, and they need to associate it with sleep. So, however tempting it is to leave them asleep in their buggy when they drop off during the day, it's better for you to shift them to their cot whenever you can. If they begin to cry when you leave the room, stay nearby and listen to see if the crying abates in the next five minutes. Sometimes it will, sometimes it won't. If it turns into hysterics, go back into the room immediately and let your presence gently soothe and comfort your baby. Stay back from the cot at first; move closer if they seem more upset, and try to comfort them without physically picking them up. Make sure they are lying on their back, and then gently stroke them. Try to remain as calm as possible, as babies pick up on your stress levels. Switch on a musical mobile, if you have one, and make soothing sounds. When they have calmed down, once again remove yourself from the room. If the crying continues, repeat the above procedure over and over. I know it's mentally exhausting, and it is so much easier to give in and pick them up, but this is the time when being patient and persistent really pays off in the long run. Generally, the first week of doing this can be very difficult; by the second week they should be settling down and getting used to the routine. If not – persevere!

Teach your baby to put themselves to sleep

SAFETY-PROOFING YOUR HOUSE

By the age of seven to eight months, your baby will start to become much more active and curious about the things around them. As their major limbs become more mobile, they are learning what are known as their large motor skills. Anything within reach will become an object of great interest, and will usually be put straight to the mouth for a quick nibble. Mobility will have begun and before you know it they will be scurrying across the floor at breakneck speed. This is something that is absolutely to be encouraged. Remember Prince Omar? When I arrived to take charge, he was so used to having everything done for him that he was practically unable to move at seven months. My first task was to encourage independent movement to exercise his muscles – and save my back! I began by making a point of insisting he be left to sit on a nice cashmere blanket on the floor. I placed his toys at various distances away from him and then called his name out loud to encourage him to stretch and lean forward to reach for them. I also shifted his position, popping him on to his knees, for example, to encourage him to crawl forwards, sideward or indeed backwards as some babies do. We did these exercises several times a day, and within days he had learned to sit up by himself, fully turn over and crawl. (Babies are usually able to sit up without assistance between six and nine months.)

Baby-proof now

At the same time as encouraging your baby and allowing them the freedom to roam and explore, it is important to be aware of household dangers. Now is the time for baby-proofing and making sure that simple accidents can be avoided and that all harmful things are kept out of their way. Don't go over the top, however. When Prince Omar's parents saw him moving around, they presented him with tailor-made knee, elbow and shoulder pads, along with a crash helmet, to ensure his safety at all times. I very diplomatically explained to them that the shagpile carpet he was put down upon, not forgetting the cashmere blanket, was sufficient padding to ensure an injury-free landing. You don't need to go over the top and empty your entire house – it's important that you leave some things for your baby to discover and explore. However, there are certain things you can do to make sure your little one stays out of harm's way.

MISS POPPY'S SAFETY-PROOFING LIST

Install smoke alarms and mini fire extinguishers, especially in the kitchen

Cover all electric sockets with safety plugs

Gate all stairs and dangerous access points

All gas, electric or open fires should be protected by a sturdy fireguard

All rugs should be secured so that they don't slip

Cover sharp edges on tables, chairs and other furniture with foam and masking tape

Fasten securely all dangling cables, curtain strings and lamp cords or put them out of your baby's reach

Fit cupboards, especially kitchen and bathroom cupboards, with safety locks

Restrict access to hot radiators, ovens and hobs

Be aware of hot water, and adjust your water temperature accordingly

Be aware of hot food and milk, especially if using a microwave which heats unevenly. Stir, shake and taste before feeding

Put the changing mat on the floor if you have a wriggler. Frisky babies can throw themselves off a changing table.

BABY BLUES

'All things pass ... patience attains all it strives for.'
– MOTHER TERESA

During your baby's first year of life, they will grow and achieve an enormous amount. Sometimes it's easy to forget this, and one ends up expecting too much of them. We must not lose sight of the fact that they are just little babies, still fully reliant upon you, and still in need of great care, comfort, patience and understanding. All babies are different and are born with individual characteristics that we cannot control, only nurture and guide. A very funny paediatrician I once met told me his standard reply to parents who came to him with sleep problems was, 'If you wanted something that would let you sleep through the night, then you should have got a fish.'

It always astonishes me what a mother goes through during the first year of a baby's life. After nine months of carrying it, she gives birth and begins an extraordinary journey of getting to know her baby and adapting herself to motherhood and all the joys and difficulties it involves. Mix that with ever-changing hormones and pure exhaustion, it is no surprise that some women suffer from what is known as post partum depression (PPD). It can be quite severe; if it is, it should be treated professionally. Don't be afraid to ask for help if you feel a sense of persistent sadness, or suffer uncontrollable crying fits and fluctuations of mood. Inability to sleep and lack of appetite are other symptoms that can creep up on you. Watch closely for these warning signs, and speak to a doctor if you feel you may be suffering from them.

'Baby blues' are a less severe form of depression. This does not mean, however, that they are not very difficult for anybody who suffers from them. They are a natural reaction to those huge mental and physical adjustments that have been made as you become a mother. Practically all the mothers I have worked with have confided in me feelings of angst, rejection and confusion; they worry that they are not bonding with this little stranger they have brought into the world; and they feel pressured to fall instantly in love with this little person they do not even know. I always tell them the same thing: love grows through the process of taking care of somebody and getting to know each other day by day. It will help more than you can imagine to talk to people – your partner, family or friends – about how you are feeling. And if you are desperate for some time alone, don't feel guilty about it. Ask someone to take care of your child, even if it's just for a couple of hours, so that you can take care of your own needs for a while.

Don't be afraid to ask for help

Most importantly, don't feel pressured by competitive parenting. There is no point comparing yourself to other mothers – you are your own individual, and you know your child's needs and limits. You will mother as you feel right, not according to what you believe others expect of you.

There will be times when you don't quite know what to do. You may be suffering from sheer exhaustion and fearing that this difficult stage will never pass. Well I can assure you it will – and far too quickly. Always remember tomorrow is another day, another opportunity for you to try again to introduce them to solids, or get them to sleep through the night, or create a routine. I fully believe that if you listen to your first natural instinct, it will guide you into doing what's right for your baby and you. There is no perfect solution to all your baby's blues, but here are a few suggestions below to keep you both smiling.

MISS POPPY'S CALMING CURES FOR BABY

Soothing music: sing or hum a lullaby, or put on a CD – Mozart and Bach seem to be babies' favourites

Motion and movement: rock and cuddle your baby, or try baby massage

Baby swaddling: wrap and cuddle for comfort

Water: give your baby a relaxing bath and sprinkle a drop of camomile or lavender oil into the water to encourage calmness

A change of scenery: pop them in the pram and go for a walk

You will also find that you and your baby will cope with the rigours of the day much more successfully if you make an effort to meet other mothers and babies. Parks are great social places to meet people and make new friends, both for you and your baby. Another fantastic way of meeting other new parents is through your local NCT (National Childbirth Trust). And most community centres or gyms have a mother-and-baby group at least once a week. It's healthy to put yourself out there and share your childrearing dilemmas with others, pick up a few tips, make some new friends and have a bit of a giggle. The social factor alone is of enormous benefit to the well-being of both of you, and a wonderful way for babies to begin learning their social skills and get used to being around other babies and grown-ups.

MISS POPPY'S TIPS FOR WORKING MUMS (AND DADS!)

As a nanny, my life revolves solely around babies and children, so I am able to devote my entire day to the care and well-being of my charges. I applaud those people who manage to raise children while holding down a full-time job. It takes tremendous energy and commitment to balance work and family life, and I have always admired parents who can do both. There are many types of childcare for you to choose from, and these are discussed on page 199 onwards. In addition, having observed working parents, I have a few good tips that will help you juggle all the demands on your time, and cope with the emotional strain that can be involved.

Feel proud of yourself. Choosing to hold down a career and have a family is a brave move, but you will find it incredibly fulfilling.

Be prepared for moments of doubt and pangs of yearning. These are very normal feelings to have as you return to work. Talk them over with other working mothers. Decide if you are going to continue breastfeeding once you return to work. If so, prepare your child in advance by introducing breast milk in a bottle at least four weeks before you return to work. Practise expressing breast milk in advance so that you may continue doing so at work.

Don't miss out. Try to give yourself at least an hour a day with your baby when you get home in the evenings: your child will love it, and it's a great way to unwind after a busy day at work.

Choose a bedtime that suits both your schedules

Make a special early-morning ritual, even if it is just a ten-minute breakfast. Read a special book before you shoot off for the day, or sing a favourite nursery rhyme.

Never make a fuss about your departure. Make sure your baby is occupied with a favourite book or toy and is receiving attention from the carer.

Ask your carer to keep a daily diary of your baby's routine, including any special moments that may have happened that day.

If possible, suggest the carer brings your baby near to your place of work once a week, so you can have a lunch date.

Don't sit and fret. Call your carer as often as you need to reassure yourself.

Talk with your carer or nursery on a regular basis. Discuss your feelings and express your worries. Clear communication clears the air.

If you are feeling stressed and overwhelmed, talk about it with your partner and other working parents. You will feel less alone and more human realising that others have gone through the same set of emotions.

MISS POPPY'S GUIDE TO HAVING FUN

Entertaining your baby is one of the most enjoyable things you will ever do, and one of the most important things for your child. The more you engage with them, the more they will reward you with affection, and the faster their development will be. But it is not always something that comes naturally; some parents need to learn how to play just as much as their children do.

Don't forget to have fun!

Try giving them a wooden spoon and a saucepan to play with. What fun! What noise! A half-empty cereal box stuck shut with Sellotape also makes great sounds. A simple box will delight if they have something to empty and fill it with – perhaps an apple or a ball, as rolling objects make for great excitement. Babies need exercise, and floor work is an essential part of their growth towards a healthy physical life. A baby as young as six months can be put down on a blanket, surrounded by a few of their favourite toys and left to explore – with a close eye kept on them, of course. Gradually their natural instinct to move will kick in and they will roll, toss and tumble forwards, backwards and sideways, reaching and grabbing for whatever object has caught their attention. Soon enough they will crawl, often with great speed.

I try to give them as much time on the floor as possible. I follow them carefully to remove objects of danger out of their way, but still try to encourage their curiosity. They will head towards stairs – to them the equivalent of Everest, ready to be conquered – like bees to a honeypot. You will need to install safety gates at the top and bottom – hurdles for both of you, I'm afraid, but they will stop your little one from coming to harm. However, it is good to expose them to stairs when you are with them, as soon enough they are going to have to learn how to get up and down them. Allow them to try and climb up with you right next to them; they will soon fly up with great enthusiasm. Coming down is more difficult for them, however. You will have to teach them the art of backing down the stairs on their front by physically placing their body in the correct position and moving their legs down one step at a time. Remember they have no sense of danger, so do be careful and never leave them alone.

The following games have kept babies amused since time immemorial. Why not try them on your little one?

PEEK-A-BOO!

This can make them giggle for hours on end. Simply cover your eyes with your hands and, with as much expression as you can muster, release your hands and say 'Peek-a-boo!' You will find that as they get used to the game, they will cover their own faces with their hands and have a go themselves – to great excitement!

PAT-A-CAKE

This is not only a lot of fun, it is also good for their hand–eye coordination. Simply clap your hands together and then gently tap the palm of their hands with yours, singing along:

Pat-a-cake, pat-a-cake, baker's man
Bake me a cake as fast as you can
Pat it and prick it and mark it with a B
And put it in the oven for baby and me

THIS LITTLE PIGGY

This little piggy went to market
[Wiggle their big toe or thumb]
This little piggy stayed at home
[Move along to the next toe or finger]
This little piggy had roast beef
[Move along to the next toe or finger]
And this little piggy had none
[Move along to the next toe or finger]
And this little piggy
[Wiggle the little toe or little finger]
Cried 'wee, wee, wee' all the way home
[Move your fingers in a walking motion along the sole of
their foot, or to under their arms if using the hand]

ROUND AND ROUND THE GARDEN

This is about as old a rhyme as they come.

Round and round the garden, like a teddy bear
[Take their hand and open it palm-upwards.
Make a gentle circular motion with your finger]
One step, two steps
[Move your fingers in a walking motion up their arm]

And tickle, tickle up there
[Tickle them softly under their arms]

MISS POPPY'S LIST OF BABY'S FIRST TOYS

A baby rattle (nice and noisy, not too heavy)
A ball
A soft cuddly toy or teddy bear
A 'squeaky-squeezy' – a noisy, colourful toy that squeaks when they
squeeze it
A teething rattle or toy (one that is easily washable and can be kept
in the fridge for a cool, soothing bite)
A musical – or even a non-musical – mobile
A toy stacker

MISS POPPY'S CREATIVE CRAFTS FOR BABIES

Kitchen fun: let your baby play with pots and pans and wooden
spoons – babies adore noise galore!
Show and tell: show your baby a picture of a dog, then bark; show
them a cat, then meow.
Sound, texture and touch: give your baby a box of pasta to shake,
an apple to roll, a magazine to shred.
Photo fun: show photos of family members – including pets – to your
baby. Point to them and call out their name.

MISS POPPY'S LIST OF FIRST BABY BOOKS

My First Board Books, published by Dorling Kindersley (with pictures
of colourful everyday objects or animals)
Peepo!, BY JANET AND ALLAN AHLBERG
Dear Zoo, BY ROD CAMPBELL

PLAYGROUPS

Playgroups tend to cater to children from the age of six months, and are generally small get-togethers of a group of mothers, fathers or carers who have children of the same age. They are good ways for both you and your child to socialise, and typically happen once or twice a week for about an hour. Often a blanket will be placed on the floor, and several toys provided for your child to explore with other children. Although they won't actually be playing together, they will enjoy babbling with, looking at and touching other children of their age. It is an excellent way for your child to learn how to socialise, and you will be amazed at how much general information you will glean from other parents about childcare, local play areas, schools and whatever else concerns you.

Some parents choose to send their children to nursery or to childcare outside the home from the age of six months, either for a couple of mornings a week or even full time. Although the norm is for children to go to nursery when they are a bit older – generally from two and a half years – there is no reason why you shouldn't choose to go down that route when they are younger. Indeed, for many parents it is a necessity, especially if Mum needs to go back to work as soon as she can. For more information on choosing suitable childcare for your little one – be it a nursery or a nanny – see the section on page 199.

CHAPTER TWO:

1–2$^1/_2$ years

> *'When I was One,*
> *I had just begun.'*
> – *Now We Are Six,* A. A. MILNE

Tots of this age have much to achieve; it will exhaust you just watching them walk and talk, sing and dance, scream and shout. They continue to grow teeth and learn how to chew food, they discover the intricacies of wearing shoes with buckles and using spoons and forks. They empty cupboards, they explore every nook and cranny, they climb mountains of stairs and learn to sit on a proper chair. Of course, they are not always on the go: they have to learn to sleep in a proper bed and not wake, they have to sit on a potty and wait, wait and wait some more. But life is never boring – when you're nearly two you have much to do ...

In this chapter we shall look at how to encourage your child through this period of constant development. As your child grows they will develop a different approach to food and meal times, so we will be looking at how to encourage them to eat a variety of healthy foods. I will explain what happens when a crawling tot becomes a toddling toddler, and what you can do to help the process along. We will then look at how their speech develops and how you can ensure that they have a good foundation for future learning. We discuss toddlers' changing sleep patterns, and how you can ensure that everyone gets a good night's sleep. As your child becomes more active and meets more children, they will also become more susceptible to illnesses, so I have included a section on the warning signs and what to do about them. Potty-training is of course an important subject for both you and your child to get to grips with, and I will be explaining how I make it as stress-free as possible. As toddlers become more active and aware, they start to learn to push their boundaries – this can result in the dreaded tantrum, and I will be offering a few ideas about how to avoid them when you can, and deal with them when you can't. It is at around this age that siblings might come into the frame; if this is the case it is important that you consider how you will deal with this big change in your toddler's – and your – life, and my experience has given plenty of good ideas about how you should go about this. Finally, there are more ideas about how to make sure your toddler's life is as fun and active as you can make it.

TUCK FOR TODDLERS

By the age of one, your child should be thoroughly enjoying a variety of healthy, nutritious, well-balanced foods served at regular meal times throughout the day. I always eat with my charges – how else would they learn such delectable table manners? But seriously, it is *Include your* important to eat with your child so that they can understand how to *baby at the* behave properly at the table, and learn the pleasure and enjoyment *meal table* of meal times in general. So pull their high chair or booster seat up to the table and make them feel included and welcome. Children love to feel they are part of the action.

Of course, it is unrealistic to expect busy parents to eat with their children three times a day, but why not take a step in the right direction by having breakfast together. Children of this age are wide awake and at their brightest first thing in the morning, and you will be surprised how sharing a bowl of cereal or a piece of toast together – even if it's just for ten minutes – can make a big difference to your child's day. If you have to rush off to work, share a short story together over breakfast. Make it a ritual: toast, cereal and story, just the two of you – it will be ten minutes that will make your child feel loved and special, and it will probably make you feel loved and special, too!

I always try to keep meal times quiet and calm by keeping distractions to a minimum. For example, I let the answering machine pick up any telephone calls. If the doorbell rings, always take your child with you to answer the door – never leave them alone at the table eating as choking can occur. Even if you are just having a snack – a cup of tea for you and a drink of juice and an apple for them – you can practice eating together at the table. Snacks are also a good time to introduce new raw sliced vegetables and fruits: if they see you eating it and enjoying it, they will want to try it too. One needs to be very patient as far as food goes with children of this age. They do not like to rush as they are extremely busy discovering different tastes and textures of foods and mastering the art of self-feeding. This should be continually encouraged by giving them their very own spoon to feed themselves; do keep one of your own and sneak in mouthfuls if they seem to be becoming frustrated by their own attempts.

Don't mind the mess

Don't be alarmed by the mess your child makes when they are eating, nor by the fact that they seem to be able to get food into nooks and crannies that you never knew existed. I have seen children absolutely encrusted in shepherd's pie from head to toe and whom

I have had to hose down before doing anything else with them. Don't worry: it's all part of the learning process and, like all stages, it eventually passes. You should be encouraged by their independence – please don't attempt to stop them just because of the mess.

Food will be thrown. It is not necessarily naughtiness at this age, but should most definitely not be encouraged. The best thing is to try to ignore it: quietly wipe it up, remove it and take it as a sign that boredom is setting in and meal time is well and truly over. Remove the rest of their food, wipe their hands and face clean and take them down from the table with as little fuss as possible.

Around the age of fifteen to twenty months, you will find the more adventurous child will attempt to climb out of their high chair or may not even physically fit any more. Now would be a good time to introduce the booster seat – a seat enhancer that can be attached to a regular chair and that puts them at a more comfortable level while they are seated at the table. A couple of firm cushions or safely attached telephone directories can do the trick nicely if you are away from home. You will need to sit with your child while they become proficient at embarking and disembarking from the booster chair – it's a long way down to the floor, and the newly discovered freedom might prove tempting to explore. If your child seems nervous about the booster chair at first, put it on the floor and let them sit on it and play with it for a while. You can even serve them a snack while they sit in it to make them feel more comfortable and help them to begin associating it with food and meal times. You may find that while they are at the table, they continually want to climb up and down – remember, it's all a bit of a novelty at first. Let them do so a couple of times and then just remove the food from the table each time they get down. That way they will learn that once they choose to disembark, the meal time is over. They will soon learn to stay sitting.

Introduce a booster seat at fifteen to twenty months

ENGLISH NANNY (CUTE UNIFORM A PLUS) REQUIRED
FOR HOLLYWOOD MOVIE-STAR FAMILY. TWINS AGED
TWO YEARS NEED TAMING, FEEDING AND GROOMING.
SEPARATE NURSERY TRAILER PROVIDED WITH OWN
GYMNASIUM, SAUNA AND STEAM ROOM.

Ally B and Hal Jr were two peas in a pod. It was like looking
after a double version of the same person: not only did they
look alike, they thought alike, laughed alike and, more
importantly, refused to eat alike. They seemed to have
worked their way through quite a few nannies before I
arrived on location, and they gave a whole new meaning to
the term 'terrible twos'. Their parents were desperate.

I had been called in to cope with a specific problem the twins
were having which worried their parents terribly. According
to Mum and Dad, the twins were starving themselves to death.
Now, one glance at these two healthy-looking children told
me that somewhere, somehow, they were getting enough
food to live on. Unfortunately I found out that they were
being nourished under the golden arches of McDonald's.

I always make a point of observing the family for a first week
before offering alternative suggestions, and in my time I've
seen it all. But even I was surprised by this family. The poor
parents had exhausted themselves trying to entice the twins
to eat. Meal times had become, much to the twins' delight,
almost literally a circus: I watched as the parents performed
comedy sketches, back flips and other gymnastic acts in order
to persuade Ally B and Hal Jr to eat a spoonful of food. But
mere crawling around on the floor making animal noises
didn't work for these two. They wanted the real thing – live
animals. A friendly animal trainer had been employed to

entertain the twins while the parents tried to coerce them into eating. On one occasion he brought an elephant into their garden, which may have been a cause for excitement and elation, but it did not seem to stimulate their appetites one little bit. A real monkeys' tea party had the twins squealing in delight as each monkey poured tea over the others' heads and it ended in a rather splendid food fight; but it was hardly a perfect example of good table manners, and it was, of course, duly copied immediately at the twins' next meal time.

The interesting thing was I never saw the twins' parents sit down to eat at a table; I didn't see them eat at all, for that matter. They were obsessed with food but never seemed to eat it themselves, always claiming to be on some new fad diet. Ally B and Hal Jr knew they had a good thing going: they thoroughly enjoyed the enormous amounts of attention lavished upon them at meal times, and they knew it would end with a trip to the golden arches. I soon nipped that little road trip in the bud: McDonald's was to be for special treats only. And the entertainment was to be saved for birthday parties only. As you may imagine, this was not greeted too kindly by my little charges. But transitional times take endless patience, time and commitment, and the twins' parents backed me all the way.

The first step was to try and get them to sit at a table. This was greeted with great shrieks of horror. I quickly put on my thinking cap and fetched a small child-size table down from their rooms, along with two little chairs. I enlisted the help of Ally B and Hal Jr by explaining that they were going to have a tea party; they became very excited when I explained that it was to be held in their very own tree house. We laid the table with Ally B's little china tea set, which she had never been allowed to play with before -- I promised to keep a close eye on it. I gave Ally B a small carton of milk to fill and refill the tiny teapot, which she did many times over and drank a good deal of fresh milk in the process. Hal Jr helped Miss Poppy in the kitchen and seemed quite enthused by the feast of fresh free-range chicken legs, chunks of cheese, carrot sticks, yellow pepper sticks and two hard-boiled eggs. I added some fresh wholemeal bread and apple slices, we packed it all up in a little picnic basket and I helped him carry it up to the tree house. Much to my amazement, the two of them sat at the table, ever so cutely, and devoured the whole lot in complete silence. Hal took his turn at filling and refilling the teapot with milk, even drinking it out of the tiny spout. I didn't interfere, but just sat back and let them get on with it. It was the first step in introducing healthy food as fun.

I allowed them the freedom of eating in the tree house several more times, and even provided a washing-up bowl with warm soapy water to wash their dishes. The next stage was to get them to sit at the kitchen table to eat along with Miss Poppy. I made a game out of it by setting their places with attractive place settings: a plastic place mat with animals on it for Hal Jr, and one with colourful letters on it for Ally B. I also found some funky plastic drinking cups with crazy straws attached to them, brightly coloured napkins and some novelty dishes with Beatrix Potter rabbits all over them – another item that was only used for decor. Instead of piling their plates with a big dollop of fish pie, I began by offering small, bite-size amounts of cubed chicken and meat on tiny skewers – a sort of mini kebab. I also made some vegetable ones with a cube of carrot, a floret of broccoli, a piece of courgette (zucchini) and even a pea skewered on the end. Dessert was followed by a mini kebab of pineapple, peach,

orange and apple. I didn't pay much attention to what was eaten first, or in what order, as my main goal was to see them eat full stop. If they refused something I didn't make a fuss, but just removed it from their plates. And I never worried that they were not eating enough because I would offer them several healthy snacks of slices of cheese, berries, wholemeal bread, fruit and vegetables throughout the day.

Food was introduced as fun to Ally B and Hal Jr – it was the only way to win them over – and once they started enjoying meal times and the fresh, healthy foods that went with it, more formal manners could be introduced, such as learning to excuse themselves from the table. We kept meal times as calm and quiet as we could with a couple of two-year-olds – no TV, no elephants, no back flips, no butlers. Their parents joined them once a day. The twins would eat a meal, and the parents drank their revolting diet shake, this time much to the childrens' horror. One day Hal Jr decided he wanted to taste it. 'Yuk!' he pronounced. And that was the end of that particular fad diet – much to everyone's delight!

By the age of fourteen months, your child should be drinking water, milk and watered-down fruit juices from a beaker or cup with a lid on. Bottles should be discouraged and cups without lids should be used as much as possible, but with lots of help from you and only while they are sitting at the table. Small cups with handles at the side or plastic beakers are your best option. Stay away from glass for obvious reasons. Offer liquids constantly through out the day, especially water if it's hot – children easily dehydrate and forget to drink when they are busy playing, so it's up to you to remember to offer a drink of water as often as you can. Stay away from all fizzy drinks – they are full of sugar and caffeine – and water all juices down as some can be as high in sugar as fizzy drinks. I have found that if you salvage a colourful plastic bottle and fill it up with water, toddlers will drink it because of the colour of the bottle alone. Trips to the park are much more fun if you get to drink out of a colourful plastic bottle!

Introduce a beaker or cup at fourteen months

You no longer have to prepare your child's food separately, as they should now be eating the same fresh, healthy foods as you. When preparing grown-up food, remove simple cooked meats and fish before seasoning with sauces, creams, spices or heavy flavourings. Set them aside for your child along with some fresh vegetables. Once you get into the habit, it becomes easier than cooking two separate meals. Salt is not needed on your toddler's food at all – and you don't need too much on yours, for that matter. Try to get into the habit of seasoning with fresh herbs and oils instead of salt and butter.

Keep portions small

Keep food portions small at meal times, because if you overload their plate you will probably just find that the food is used for sculpting, squishing and throwing rather than eating. Best to serve smaller bite-size portions and let them ask for seconds if they want it. Instead, your child should also be enjoying a wide selection of healthy snacks throughout the day, to complement their three meals and sustain their energy levels, otherwise they will become tired and grumpy. It doesn't need to be anything too much: a selection of finger foods such as slices of fresh fruit, vegetable sticks, wholemeal breadsticks, salt-free crackers, a piece of cheese or a cube of chicken. Healthy snacks are a necessary part of a toddler's diet as they tend to eat little and often.

As far as the other type of snack goes (you know what I mean – sweets, chocolate, crisps and biscuits) try not to give them too freely or they will just develop a craving for sugar and salt, and all your hard work will go straight out of the window. It is inevitable that your child will consume some sort of sweet snacks – at birthday parties, for example – but as long as healthy snacks are the norm, the occasional treats are nothing to worry about. I have observed children deprived from any sweet treats at all who then arrive at a birthday party and go absolutely berserk, not wanting to leave the table until each and every chocolate biscuit and crumb of cake is consumed. Always remember to brush your child's teeth after eating sweets. It's a good habit to start early.

There will be times when your tot simply refuses to eat, or becomes fussy about certain foods they seemed to demolish just yesterday. They might choose to replace food with milk – endless amounts of it. Don't take it too seriously; it really is just a passing phase. *Don't make* Whatever you do, try not to turn it into a battlefield. You will lose, *meals a* hands down. If your child simply refuses food and replaces it with *battlefield* milk, give it a week and then begin to cut back on the amount of milk given and water it down if necessary in order to increase their appetite. (Your child should be given full-fat milk up until the age of two years; it should then be replaced with semi-skimmed (2%) milk, but not skimmed (skim) as it is too watery.) It may seem like they are not eating any vegetables at all, but they are probably just going through a phase of preferring fruit, which is just as good for them. You will see how they change from one food group to another. If they insist on eating only yogurt three times a day for an entire week, let them. The less attention you give it, the quicker it will pass. And somehow children have a way of establishing a balanced diet if you offer a selection of fresh, healthy foods.

The only-drinking-milk stage is fairly common. If your child is teething, their gums can be very sensitive to certain textures; at such times they often prefer liquid foods like milk and fresh juices, which can be made from vegetables as well as fruits. If you are lucky enough to have a juicer, now's the time to use it; if not, blenders can work wonders as long as you strain the juice after you have blended it. In fact, making carrot juice is a favourite pastime for all the toddlers I have cared for – the best bit being that they can drink it after the fun and games of preparing it. It is also great fun mixing flavours. Carrot too bitter? Add a little apple or mango to sweeten. What could be healthier or more nutritious? My charges have enjoyed quite a splendid choice of cocktails, as they called them – we pop in chunks of floating fruit or vegetables, or add a bit more pzazz by creating a fruit skewer with pieces of fruit and vegetables and even a maraschino cherry. If there's not time for preparing your own, you can buy many different organic juices and vegetable drinks from health-food stores and supermarkets. Just make sure they are pasteurised so as not to give tummy upsets; and always water them down as some contain far too much sugar.

Smoothies are another great way to get your child to eat vegetables and fruits. Simply throw some fruit or vegetables of your choice into a blender, add a little ice or milk (ice-cream or frozen yogurt for special treats) and blend. Children particularly love the texture of the crunchy ice, and it can help soothe the gums if they are swollen from teething. Just make sure it is well crushed to prevent choking. If the smoothies need it, add a tiny spot of maple syrup to sweeten.

Try to serve food in simple portions. Place a few veggies on one side of the plate, a few pieces of fish, chicken or meat in another separate pile and some potato, rice or pasta on another part of the plate. They like to see the differences in food rather than one great pile of mush. Serve meals on any interesting-shaped dishes you *Use* might have. I knew one little girl who refused to eat out of *interesting* anything but the goldfish bowl. I am always happy to oblige *dishes* within reason, so we upgraded Sally the goldfish to slightly *and plates* smarter accommodation in a larger rectangular tank, washed the goldfish bowl several times in the dishwasher, then served our little mermaid her food out of it. She was delighted and her appetite increased tenfold. It caused much amusement from any visitors, who must have thought the new nanny was slightly eccentric to say the least. The point is that you should be broad-minded and inventive, and your kids will love it.

RECIPES FROM MISS POPPY'S PANTRY

All these recipes are suitable for children from twelve months.

HONEY BEAR PORRIDGE
50g (2oz) organic oats
150ml (5floz) milk
a tiny pinch of salt
a drop of honey from the honey bear

Place the oats, milk and salt into a saucepan and bring to the boil, stirring constantly for 5–6 minutes until it reaches a thick con-sistency. Pour into a breakfast bowl and allow your child to drizzle honey on top. You can buy honey in plastic bear-shaped pots, which are fun; otherwise you will need to make sure that a teddy bear is around to supervise the amount of honey he's willing to lend from his pot!

BOILED EGG AND BACON SOLDIERS
1 fresh free-range egg
4 strips organic back bacon

Pre-heat the grill to high. Trim any excess fat from the bacon with scissors, leaving behind lean strips of meat. Place on a baking tray and grill each side for 3–4 minutes until nice and crispy. Leave to cool.

Meanwhile, place the egg in a pan of boiling water and boil for 3½ minutes. Draw a smiley face on the shell, and serve the egg in a novelty or elegant eggcup.

Allow your child – with help if needed – to smash and peel the top of the egg in order to march their bacon soldiers into the yummy yellow yolk.

YOGURT MIX AND MATCH
a squeeze of honey or maple syrup
a scoop of fresh muesli or granola
stewed apples
fresh berries or chopped pieces of fresh fruit
a scoop of organic cereal
plain organic yogurt

Pour each ingredient into a small pot, ramekin or cup-cake case, with the exception of the yogurt, which you should place in a slightly larger breakfast-cereal-size bowl and surround it with all the other pots. Simply let your child choose which toppings and flavours they would like to create their very own original yogurt – or 'magic potion', as one of my former charges liked to call it. This is excellent for picky eaters.

MORNING SMOOTHIE
150ml (5floz) milk
150ml (5floz) plain organic yogurt
2 of the following fruits:
pineapple
banana
strawberries
apple
mango
peaches
pears
oranges
blueberries
kiwi
dribble of honey or maple syrup
a handful crushed ice
apple or orange juice (optional)

Place all the ingredients in a blender and whiz. For a slightly thinner texture, add a splash of apple or orange juice. Serve in an ice cream sundae glass with a straw and a long spoon.

WHOLEWHEAT PASTA SALAD

225g (8oz) medium-sized wholewheat pasta shells
1 large tomato, finely chopped
2 tablespoons chopped cucumber, finely chopped
1 stick celery, finely chopped
1 ripe avocado, finely chopped
a small tin of cooked red kidney beans, drained
2 tablespoons chopped cooked green beans
175g (6oz) chopped cooked chicken or a small tin of tuna
3–4 tablespoons olive oil
1–2 tablespoons balsamic vinegar
a squeeze of lemon juice

Boil the pasta shells for 8–10 minutes until tender, drain, then run the cooked pasta shells under cold water for 1 minute. Set aside to cool. In a large mixing bowl mix the tomato, cucumber, celery, avocado, kidney beans, green beans and chicken or tuna. Add the cool pasta shells. Make a dressing to taste from the oil and vinegar, mix into the salad then squeeze a little lemon juice on top and serve.

RICE WITH VEGETABLES

3 tablespoons finely chopped vegetables – you could use carrots,
    peas, courgettes or yellow or orange peppers
1 tablespoon olive oil
125g (4½oz) cooked brown rice

Sauté the vegetables in the olive oil for 2–3 minutes until softened. Add the brown rice and mix together. This is good served with skewered salmon or chicken cubes.

COMFORTING CHICKEN SOUP

1 small chicken, cut into approximately 8 pieces
  (ask your butcher to do this for you)
1 large onion
4 carrots
2 celery stalks, with green leaves
1 medium turnip
2.75 litres (5 pints) cold water
2 sprigs parsley
1 sprig thyme
salt and pepper
225g (8oz) wholewheat pasta

Rinse the chicken pieces. Peel the onion and cut into rough chunks. Scrub the carrots, leaving the skin intact. Rinse the celery and break each stalk into two pieces. Peel and roughly chop the turnip.

In a large saucepan bring the water to the boil. Add the chicken pieces, onion, carrot, celery, turnip, parsley and thyme. Cover the pan and bring the water back to the boil. Remove any scum from the surface and discard. Turn down the heat and leave to simmer gently for 2 hours, skimming the surface every so often. Leave to cool and season with salt and pepper. Strain the stock into a large clean pan, using a muslin cloth or tea towel placed inside a large strainer. Pick out the chicken pieces and set aside the carrot and turnip. Discard the onion, celery and herbs.

Now that the chicken is cooked pull the meat off the bones and add it to the strained stock. Chop the carrot and turnip into smaller pieces and add those also. Bring the chicken broth to the boil and add the pasta, boiling until the pasta is tender. Skim off any chicken fat that may rise to the top, and serve. (The chicken soup, without the pasta, can be frozen and used when needed.)

VEGETABLE PASTA

125g (4oz) wholewheat pasta such as spaghetti or penne
selection of fresh vegetables such as broccoli, cauliflower, baby
    sweetcorn or snow peas
2 tablespoons cottage cheese
1 tablespoon olive oil

Bring a pan of water to the boil and cook the pasta until tender.
Meanwhile, prepare and chop the vegetables into bite-size chunks.
In a frying pan heat the olive oil and sauté the vegetables for 4-5
minutes until tender. Toss the pasta with the cottage cheese and
vegetables. For added protein, you could also toss in some shredded
cooked chicken or tofu.

CHICKEN DRUMSTICKS

1 tablespoons olive oil
1 teaspoon fresh or dried mixed herbs
fresh lemon juice
2–4 organic chicken drumsticks

Pre-heat the oven to 200°C/400°F/Gas Mark 6. Mix the olive oil,
herbs and lemon juice together and rub the mixture on to the
chicken drumsticks. Place in a baking dish and bake for 35–40
minutes until cooked and golden.

HONEYDEW MELON DELIGHT

half a honeydew melon
2 tablespoons cottage cheese

Scoop out the melon with a melon baller and set the melon balls
aside. Place the cottage cheese inside the melon and hide the
melon balls in the cottage cheese – much fun will be had digging
the melon balls out.

COTTAGE TOAST

1 slice wholemeal brown bread
2 soaked, dried apricots, or a freshly chopped peach
1 tablespoon pasteurised cottage cheese

Toast the bread. Meanwhile, chop the apricot or fresh peach into tiny pieces and mix together with the cottage cheese.

Spread the toast with the cottage cheese mixture and cut into bite-size squares.

CHEESE ON TOAST

1 slice wholemeal bread
2 tablespoons grated cheddar cheese
2 cherry tomatoes

Pre-heat the grill to high and toast the bread on one side only. Place the grated cheese on the untoasted side and pop back under the grill until the cheese bubbles. Cut into four quarters, leave to cool slightly and serve with half a cherry tomato on top of each piece.

FRUIT CRUMBLE

225g (8oz) fruit in season, or frozen fruit
1 tablespoon honey or maple syrup
½ teaspoon cinnamon
50g (2oz) self-raising flour
75g (3oz) porridge oats
50g (2oz) demerara sugar
40g (1½oz) cold butter, cubed

Pre-heat the oven to 200°C/400°F/Gas Mark 6. Place the fruit and honey or maple syrup into a pan and heat gently, stirring constantly. Transfer to a bowl of about 3cm (1in) in depth and sprinkle the cinnamon on top. To make the topping, place all the other ingredients into a mixing bowl and crumble together using only your fingertips until the mixture resembles breadcrumbs. Scatter over the fruit and bake for 25 minutes until the top is golden and crisp. Serve with frozen yogurt, ice cream or fromage frais.

MISS POPPY'S TIPS FOR FUSSY NON-EATERS

Do not worry! They will not starve, it's a passing phase

Offer them a selection of small, bite-size foods rather than one big meal

Make sure the selection includes enticing, brightly coloured foods such as fruits and vegetables

Supply plenty of drinks, particularly in hot weather: water, diluted fruit juices and smoothies

Reduce or water down their milk intake if they are replacing food with milk.

Remember that children tend to chop and change between different foods. Fruits provide as much goodness as vegetables; cheese and eggs provide as much protein as meat

Never force food or make an issue if they don't eat something; children eat what they need

Provide healthy nutritious snacks when needed

Be innovative and creative, and serve food in different ways

MISS POPPY'S GUIDE TO EATING OUT

Eating out with your toddler is perfectly possible if you are prepared and realistic. A five-course meal at the Ritz may be a little far-fetched just at the moment, but many restaurants do cater for and encourage you to bring along small children. The trick is to keep it short and sweet.

When choosing a restaurant, call ahead and ask if they have a high chair or booster seat so that you don't have to bring your own.

If you forget, don't worry: a few telephone directories or pillows can usually be dug up from somewhere. Choose your dining time wisely by making sure your child isn't absolutely starving and tired at the exact time of your restaurant booking. Seat them near a window if there is one so that they have something fun to look at, or choose an area where you can easily manoeuvre them in and out without disturbing fellow diners. Bring along a favourite small, quiet toy, a book or a few crayons and paper to amuse them – remember it's very hard for a toddler to be expected to sit still for a long period of time.

Often there will be a basket of bread or some breadsticks to tide them over, but to be safe it is a good idea to bring along a few snacks in case service is slow or the restaurant is busy. Also pack a favourite drinking cup and spoon, and don't forget a bib. Order for your child immediately. Don't choose anything too fancy – a child-size portion of a simple starter, or a plate of plain pasta with vegetables. If they seem restless, take them outside to stretch their legs before the food arrives; if they seem downright intent on causing a fuss, better to just take them home and try again next time. I do believe, however, the only way to teach children how to behave in various social situations is to make sure they are exposed to them as early as you can. Be aware of their limits, though, and act accordingly. Don't expect too much too soon.

TODDLING TOTS

'A child reminds us that playtime
is an essential part of our daily routine.'
— ANONYMOUS

All children start to walk at different ages, and it can be anywhere from twelve to eighteen months before your tot decides to get around on two legs instead of four. The speed at which some toddlers crawl can be quite astounding, and if they are managing to cover large areas quickly, they might not even attempt to walk upright for some time. I have seen ten-month-old walkers as well as children who have chosen to crawl up until the age of eighteen months. The point is that they all walk eventually, so please be patient and allow your child to follow his or her own timing.

The first indication that a child is preparing to walk is when they begin pulling themselves up on pieces of furniture such as a low coffee table or the legs of a chair. Standing up is a mighty feat for them at this stage. They wobble and shake, and once they are up they have to plop down – but it's usually a soft landing on a padded nappy. They will be delighted with their progress and look to you for praise and recognition. Smile, clap and convey your delight in any way you can.

Try placing an interesting object such as a favourite toy on the other side of the coffee table as a challenge. To help, you can take both of their hands and walk them around to the other side to retrieve it. Do this a few times and eventually they will begin to shuffle their way around the table on their own, stabilising themselves with their hands on the table and shuffling their feet. *Cruising is the prelude to walking* This is called cruising, and is an the intermediary stage between being able to stand up alone and actually being able to walk. Sofas are also ideal for cruising along. Start them at one end and put something enticing at the other end to encourage them to walk along. Often they just like to lean on the sofa or coffee table to practise standing up, and this eventually leads to their being able to stand unaided. Be prepared for a few bumps and bruises during this stage, and try not to overreact when they do fall or else they will start to share your fear and anxiety and may stop attempting to walk for a while. Offer them lots of kisses and cuddles, but then let them get back on with it.

Tots love to take hold of both your hands or your fingers and stand up, slowly swinging their hips into tiny steps forward – first one then two. Arrange a few chairs or low tables for them to pull themselves up, lean on and learn to toddle around. Standing up alone is a mighty feat for them at this stage. Help them by holding on to their hands and then, once they are stable, let go – but remain

right next to them to catch them as they fall. Once they are able to stand unaided, the business of getting back down to the ground may involve a lot of wobbling and shaking, and will probably end with a sudden plop back down to the floor. When they are able to stand up alone, stand a few feet in front of them, hold out your hands and encourage them to walk forward towards you and fall into your arms for a big cuddle.

All my charges have enjoyed push-along toys, be it a stuffed animal on wheels or a trolley full of building blocks – anything with a handle so that they can lean on it as they walk along. Not only are they a source of a great deal of fun, they also help tremendously with walking skills. You will see by their smile what an enormous sense of achievement they derive from such simple tasks. It gives them the confidence to take those first few steps alone.

To start with they are only able to walk in a straight line – no turning corners or bending down, just lots of wobbling with their arms stretched out like something out of an old Frankenstein movie. By the age of eighteen months to two years, however, their technique will have developed into something much more masterful: they are able to bend at the knees, pick up items to carry, navigate corners, walk backwards and climb upstairs. Try to give them space to explore, such as an area in or outside the house, which is safe, non-slippery and protected from sharp corners or loose, hanging cables and curtain cords. Before you know it they will be toddling around everywhere with amazing confidence.

While there is no need to be overzealous and panicked if your child shows no interest in attempting to learn how to walk, it is important that you should be offering them plenty of space and equipment so that they can practise. A child plonked in a playpen all the time will never learn to move freely in such a cramped space.

Most importantly, try not to force the issue, and remember that their development is often hereditary, so if you were a late walker, the chances are your child will also be. If, however, they are not walking by the age of eighteen to twenty months, mention it to your doctor who may refer you to a specialist.

Learning to walk is of course rather more than simply a matter of putting one foot in front of the other. Balance, coordination and a general awareness of how their body moves are all essential concepts for toddlers to get to grips with at an early age, and there are plenty of ways that you can help them do this.

Children love small chairs that are just the right size for them to get in and out of, and this is an excellent exercise in bending at the knees. Dancing to music is another excellent way of encouraging them to become aware of their bodies and increase their coordination. If you dance for your child, they will copy you in their own way, and they will soon learn to dance by themselves when they hear music. Singing songs and nursery rhymes with accompanying actions will also help to encourage balance and coordination – but more importantly both you and they will have a lot of fun.

MISS POPPY'S ACTION NURSERY RHYMES
I'M A LITTLE TEAPOT

I'm a little teapot, short and stout
[Stand with your hands on your hip]
Here is my handle, here is my spout
[Keep one hand on your hip and
bend your other arm into a spout shape]
When I get all steamed up, I will shout
Tip me over and pour me out
[Lean over to mimic pouring tea out of the spout]

RING-A-RING O' ROSES

Ring-a-ring o' roses
[Hold hands, drop down to the child's level and
move around in a circle]
A pocket full of posies
Atishoo! Atishoo!
[Nod your head as if you are sneezing]
We all fall down
[Collapse to the floor]

RIDE A COCK HORSE

Ride a cock horse to Banbury Cross
[Cross you legs and let them sit on your perched foot.
Hold their hands and move your foot up and
down to mimic a horse trotting]
To see a fine lady ride on a white horse
With rings on her fingers and bells on her toes
[Trot faster]
She shall have music wherever she goes

TWO LITTLE DICKY BIRDS

Two little dicky birds
Sitting on a wall
[Clench both fists, point your index fingers upwards,
then curl them up and down]
One named Peter
One named Paul
Fly away Peter
[Swing one arm behind your back hiding the finger]
Fly away Paul
[Swing the other arm behind you back]
Come back Peter
[Bring one index finger back]

Come back Paul
[Bring the other index finger back]

ITSY-BITSY SPIDER
Itsy-bitsy spider climbed the water spout
[Use your hands to imitate the action of
a spider climbing upwards]
Down came the rain and washed the spider out
[Wiggle your fingers downwards, imitating rain]
Out came the sun and dried up all the rain
[Draw a circle with your hands]
So Itsy-bitsy spider could climb the spout again.

I believe that physical pleasure and the freedom of the outdoors truly feed children's minds and bodies, giving them the opportunity to run free, roam and explore their strengths. The sights, sounds and impressions capture their imagination and curiosity. I have spent many an hour chasing squirrels with a two-year-old, or rolling down a grass bank just for the pure fun of it. Toddlers have huge amounts of energy which need channelling, and there is no better place to do this than in the great outdoors. Testing their skills on the climbing frame, kicking a ball, rolling down a hill, swinging high into the sky – these are all simple childhood delights that allow them to explore their physical capabilities, give them confidence, teach them to conquer their fears and so help them grow into healthy human beings. Moreover, all these activities help their concentration, which will benefit them hugely in their future learning.

Next time your child decides to walk on a wall, slow down and remember how good it makes them feel to be so able. Hold their hand and offer encouragement. When they spot a hill, let them run freely up it and roll down on their sides, squealing with delight.

Find a small tree and let them climb it. Several of my charges have enjoyed measuring their growth against a favourite tree in their local park. We would visit it regularly through the changing seasons and watch it blossom and grow, just like them. Children need to be allowed to get dirty. Provide play clothes purely for getting mucky, and wellington boots for rainy-day walks, splashing in the mud and jumping into puddles. There's nothing better than puddle-jumping and singing in the rain, then back home for tea, all warm and cosy, snuggled up together with a good book to read.

By the age of two years, when your tot is truly an up-and-running toddler, you will find that your speed will also have to increase as their curiosity combined with their increased mobility leads them to discover every nook and cranny in the house. Remember, it's not naughtiness, simply curiosity, so it should never be punished at this age. Just try to distract their attention with something that looks like more fun, or remove them physically from the room.

MISS POPPY'S TOP TOYS FOR TODDLERS

As your child starts learning how to toddle, anything that helps them with general coordination will be of huge value. This might include:

A push-along toy such as a horse, donkey or dog on wheels to encourage walking

A pull-along toy such as a dog, duck or car on wheels

A tricycle, car, bike or tractor with wheels to sit on and manoeuvre with their feet

A mini chair just their size for them to practise climbing in and out

Building blocks

Stacking cups or rings

An activity cube with a shape sorter

A toy workbench with a wooden hammer

A pictorial wooden puzzle

FIRST SHOES

Before they even start thinking about walking, your baby may be wearing slip-on shoes or slippers made of loose fabric – more for warmth and fashion than anything else. In fact, when babies are learning to crawl, they much prefer to be barefoot as socks and slippers can make them slide around a bit too much for their purposes, although you can buy socks and slippers with slip-resistant grips on the sole.

When you get to the point where your child is confidently standing by themselves and taking several unaided steps, you can purchase a decent pair of walking shoes. The best advice I can give you is to seek out a professional children's shoe shop in your area. Your local department store should have a children's shoe department – don't be afraid to ask for someone qualified and with experience. It is a very good investment of your time to build up a good relationship as you will be needing their help a lot in the future: you will have to replace your child's shoes every ten to twelve weeks at this stage.

You can easily spot an expert. They will measure your child's foot carefully, and will recommend a simple, sensible starter shoe over the latest fly-by-night fashion. They will spend plenty of time making sure the shoe fits well, and will ask your child to stand up straight with both shoes on so that they can measure the space between their big toe and the tip of the shoe. A thumb's width is the correct amount of space to leave for growth. Remember to take a couple of pairs of socks with you to try on with shoes, as they will affect what size you buy. The back of the shoe will be checked for space and a supportive, firm fit. There should be no harsh material to rub and cause blisters. The sole of the shoe should have grips of some sort so that it does not slip or slide. Most importantly, your child's first shoe should be comfortable.

It was once recommended that a child's first shoe should be of the type that resembles a boot, covering the ankle. In fact, this type of shoe can cause problems and should be avoided as it offers the ankle no flexibility at all. If you really like the look of that type of shoe, opt for one made of extremely soft, flexible leather that does not offer the ankle any support. Sports shoes and trainers are fine, but they do tend to make your child's feet sweat. This can lead to heat rashes as well as being rather smelly, so it's best not to let them spend all day in their trainers.

And finally, a word about something that will make shoe-wearing a great deal easier for you and your child: Velcro. Laces, buckles and bows can be a bit fussy at this stage – there will be plenty of time in the future for you teach them how to tie their shoelaces. At this age, I always opt for Velcro – in my experience it has prevented many a tantrum from a frustrated toddler who would otherwise get into a total tizzy as they start learning to put on and remove their own shoes!

CHATTERING TODDLERS

'Draw a crazy picture, write a natty poem.
Sing a mumble-gumble song, whistle through your comb.
Do a loony-goony dance cross the kitchen floor.
Put something silly in the word that ain't there before.'
— SHEL SILVERSTEIN

Toddlers chatter in their own unique way. It is the sweetest thing in the world to tiptoe into the nursery while they lie in their cot to hear them babbling away having an intense conversation with themselves. I like to call it a conversation of sounds. I have always made a point of speaking clearly and precisely to babies and young children, and I avoid any silly baby talk. It helps tremendously if you're a chatterbox like myself. It can be like having a one-way conversation, but you will have a captive audience who is listening and learning, absorbing like a sponge.

Learning to speak is like learning a new language: one learns by word association and by building up a vocabulary. A one-year-old will be listening and learning even if you think they are paying no attention whatsoever, so it is important to remember to speak to *Chatter at* them at any available opportunity, whether you are getting dressed, *every* having breakfast, going out for a stroll – they are all perfect *opportunity* opportunities for them to play and learn. Get into the habit of naming things before you give them to your child. As you serve breakfast, hand them the bowl and say 'bowl' very clearly. Do the same with the spoon, cup, apple or banana. As you are getting them dressed, name all the items of clothing before you put them on. Try and maintain eye contact with them as you do this, and repeat the word so that they have an opportunity to imitate you.

By the age of fourteen months, your toddler may start to say a few words such as 'Mama' or 'Dada'. When they do, you must always respond by saying the word properly back to them with a smile showing that you fully understand and are pleased with them. Now is not the time to correct them; instead you should encourage more attempts at verbal communication. Don't be upset either if they call Mummy 'Dada' – it's often easier to say than 'Mama'. Just be delighted that they have started communicating.

By the age of fifteen months their babbling will blossom into words of sorts, even if you are the only one who can decipher their meaning. By the age of eighteen months your toddler will love to help by fetching and carrying shoes, hats, mittens and coats. Describe the colour of the coat or hat and next time ask them to fetch their red coat or blue shoes. Then start introducing shapes –

the round apple, the square book. It might sound simple, but it will help your child's understanding of speech and learning of vocabulary enormously.

Don't expect perfection. The majority of the time words will be shortened or backwards, and often the first part of a word will be repeated until it sounds right to your child. Give them time to spit it out; give them your full attention by holding their hand and looking directly at them; most importantly, smile! You must show them that you are interested and curious about what they have to say. Make them understand that you value their time by not interrupting and answering for them. They may often repeat the first part of the word several times before they fully pronounce the word in question. When they do manage to say the whole word, repeat it back to them to confirm they have said it correctly. They will be thoroughly pleased with themselves – and so they should be.

Take time to listen

I have noticed that children who are very physically busy tend to communicate through sign language rather than words. They use their hands and facial gestures, nodding their head or shaking it vigorously to make themselves understood, rather than using their verbal skills. I put it down to the fact that they are just too busy moving around and exploring to speak. They tend to understand what you are saying, though – when you ask 'Where's Teddy?', they will run and fetch him. You certainly shouldn't worry about this. You will find that they will start saying words all of a sudden. Similarly, toddlers who have older siblings often leave the elder child to communicate on their behalf. I think the elder children rather enjoy the power of this secret way of communicating, but you can encourage the elder child to do what you are doing and to name all the items they give to their younger sibling and praise any attempt to speak.

Children learn to speak at very different ages, so do not worry if your child is not speaking fully or if you are the only person who can understand their strange speech pattern. Proper pronunciation and grammar will come by the time they are four years old, but as long you can communicate with your child and understand them, that is what is important. If you – or they – feel frustrated and they don't seem to be interested in communicating with you even non-verbally, talk to your doctor, who may suggest a hearing test.

I have found that rhythm, rhyme, song and dance play a huge part in laying the foundations for linguistic skills. They are also an excellent way to make daily chores a bit more interesting, and even help you have a giggle or two. They can also be an excellent deviation tactic in moments of great need. If your child is squirming and refusing to put on their shoes, sweep them up into your arms and sing or recite a favourite rhyme or song.

Here are a few familiar rhymes that will help your child learn simple words, followed by games to help teach them simple speech.

MISS POPPY'S HELP-ALONG RHYMES AND POEMS
The following rhymes are good for getting dressed and undressed:

DIDDLE DIDDLE DUMPLING
Diddle diddle dumpling, my son John
Went to bed with his trousers on
One shoe off, the other shoe on
Diddle diddle dumpling, my son John

ONE, TWO
One, two
Buckle my shoe
Three, four

Shut the door
Five, six
Pick up sticks
Seven, eight
Lay them straight

The following rhymes are good for meal times:

LITTLE JACK HORNER

Little Jack Horner sat in a corner
Eating a Christmas pie
He put in his thumb and pulled out a plum
And said, 'What a good boy am I!'

LITTLE TOMMY TUCKER

Little Tommy Tucker
Sings for his supper
What shall he eat?
White bread and butter
How shall he cut it
Without any knife?
How will he be married
Without any wife?

The following rhymes are good for bath time:

BATH TIME

A rubber duck and a sailing boat
I watch my bath toys sink and float
They keep me company in the tub
Till Mummy makes me soap and scrub
I love to take a bath each night
And go to bed all clean and bright

AFTER A BATH

After a bath, I try, try, try
To wipe myself till I'm dry, dry, dry
Hands to wipe, and fingers and toes
And two wet legs and a shiny nose
Just think how much less time I'd take
If I were a dog, and could shake, shake, shake!

The following rhymes are good for getting ready for bed:

GO TO BED

Go to bed first
A golden purse
Go to bed second
A golden pheasant
Go to bed third
A golden bird

WEE WILLIE WINKIE

Wee Willie Winkie runs through the town
Upstairs and downstairs in his nightgown
Rapping at the windows, crying through the locks
Are the children in their beds, for now it's eight o'clock?

MISS POPPY'S GAMES TO TEACH SPEECH
WHERE'S MY NOSE

Where's my nose? Where's your nose? Where's Teddy's nose?
[Simply ask your child to point to your nose,
then their nose, then Teddy's nose,
all the while saying the words 'nose' and 'teddy']
Where's my toes? Where's your toes? Where's Teddy's toes?
Where's my ears? Where's your ears? Where's Teddy ears?

THE PLEASE AND THANK YOU GAME

This is a wonderful game to teach manners and to practise saying the magic words please and thank you. Choose a favourite toy and simply play giving it back and forth, but say 'please' when requesting the toy and 'thank you' when the toy is received. Don't pass the toy along unless you hear the magic words – and you can always hide it behind your back or up your jumper for more of a giggle.

HEAD, SHOULDERS, KNEES AND TOES

Stand opposite each other and point to the relevant parts of the body as you sing:

Head, shoulders, knees and toes
Knees and toes
Head, shoulders, knees and toes
Knees and toes
And eyes and ears and mouth and nose
Head, shoulders, knees and toes
Knees and toes

BOOKS

Picture books are of enormous help in developing your child's vocabulary; they can even be introduced before their first year. It is wonderful gift to introduce the joy of books and reading to your toddler, and it will stay with them through life. From the age of one year they love the chunky, hardback, wear-and-tear books with distinctive pictures of everyday items like a teddy bear, a ball, a pair of shoes or a yellow duck. They are well able to turn the pages on the chunky cardboard books with their nimble fingers. Point to an item in the book like a ball, and say the word out loud. Do this over and over again – children learn through repetition and familiarity which nourishes their confidence and boosts their self-esteem. Let them go and fetch a ball for you when they see it in the book. They love to compare their teddy to the one in the

Use books to develop language

book. Animal books should be accompanied by the noises the animal makes, and your child will respond to actions and sounds that match the words or pictures.

Children gain comfort and confidence from you repeating the same story over and over again, and from knowing what is on the next page of the book. Capture their curiosity and ask them what comes next. Reading books to a child between the ages of one and two should be as interactive and fun as possible because their attention span is too short for them to sit still and concentrate for long. Be patient, and never force a child to sit still while you read; part of understanding your child is to understand their limits and capabilities. This is why it is better to start with the picture books at first. If you do choose other books, just tell a shorter version of the story by pointing to the pictures and encouraging your child to recognise them. You will find that they will have the last page turned while you are still trying to read the first, but persevere and you will find they start to have their absolute favourite books which they will have memorised word for word. Heaven forbid you miss a page, or even a word – it will be pointed out immediately. They may choose the same book night after night because it offers comfort and familiarity. Eventually, though, they will find a new book they like, and then that will become a familiar part of their bedtime routine.

MISS POPPY'S LIST OF BOOKS FOR TODDLERS
Guess How Much I Love You, BY SAM MCBRATNEY AND
   ANITA JERAM
Spot The Dog, BY ERIC HILL
The Very Hungry Caterpillar, BY ERIC CARLE
We're Going On A Bear Hunt, BY MICHAEL ROSEN AND
   HELEN OXENBURY
Go Maisy, Go!, BY LUCY COUSINS

Goodnight Moon, BY MARGARET WISE BROWN
Five Little Monkeys, BY ZITA NEWCOME
Farm Animals, BY P. DUNN
Touch and Feel Baby Animals, PUBLISHED BY DORLING
  KINDERSLEY
Brown Bear, Brown Bear, What Do You See?,
  BY BILL MARTIN JR AND ERIC CARLE

TODDLERS' NAP TIMES

'O Bed! O Bed! delicious bed!
That heaven upon earth to the weary head.'
Miss Kilmansegg – Her Dream, THOMAS TOOD

Nap time should be a well-established part of your daytime
routine, and you should both look forward to it. From the age of
one year on your child should be having one good solid nap a day,
preferably after lunch. Lunch should be fairly early for one-year-
olds – around half past eleven – and a little later for two-year-olds
– say twelve to half past. It's important not to leave lunch too late.
If you find that they don't seem interested in their food and that
they're rubbing their eyes, they are past it. Much better to put
them down for a nap now and give them lunch when they wake
up – which will probably be sooner than you think because their
tummies will be rumbling!

They should preferably sleep for about two hours – no more or
you'll find that they are reluctant to go to sleep at bedtime. You
shouldn't make a big fuss about putting them down – no hanging
around reading books at nap time, as this will just delay the
process and give them a second burst of energy. Just close the
curtains, switch on the baby monitor, put Teddy in the cot (crib)
or bed and away you go. You might hear a few yelps to start with,

[margin note:] Nap after lunch

and children of this age often like to sing themselves to sleep; you might even find that they have scrunched themselves up in a corner with their legs swinging high above them. Best to leave them be – it's just their way of relaxing and winding down after a busy morning. Eventually they will drop off to sleep. Try to keep household noises and distractions down to a minimum during nap time; if they hear you chatting away on the telephone, they will want to be with you.

It is sometimes tempting to skip naps if they seem alert and full of energy at lunch time. But at four o'clock or so they will just collapse into a heap of tiredness and then it's quite difficult to keep them awake until bedtime. If they do fall asleep later on in the afternoon, be prepared for a later bedtime. But it's much better to try and keep them up: bring bath time forward to before supper and make it extra long, as it's a good place to relax and stay calm. Then just pop them to bed a bit earlier; but bear in mind that you might have an early morning.

Once they have settled into their one-nap-a-day routine, you will find that they wake up naturally after a couple of hours. If they have had a particularly active morning, you may need to add an extra half hour on top, but don't go beyond that. If you need to wake them up, do so very gently. Go into their room and open the curtains. Lean over the cot or bed and gently stroke them. If need be, leave them for five or ten minutes to come to – it can be very disorientating waking up in the middle of the day. Some toddlers wake more easily than others. I have cared for several who woke up in the afternoon like a bear with a sore head. If you child is like that, you just have to give them a bit more time to come to. Pick them up if they allow it, and give them a cuddle; offer them a drink of water or diluted fruit juice, which will help to refresh them. Quietly discuss what you are going to do in the afternoon –

if they know they are going to the sandpit, it's amazing how it can motivate them to wake up!

SWEET DREAMS

'There is a time for many words, and there is also a time for sleep.'
– The Odyssey, HOMER

Never underestimate the power of sleep. Think of it like petrol for the car: without it, the car won't run. Sleep is fuel that powers the mind. As we discussed in the previous chapter, a good bedtime routine is essential; it is the key to your little one blossoming into an intelligent, healthy, happy child.

My charges have always looked forward to bedtime. They associate it with warmth, calm, comfort and lots of cuddles. Bed is a place where they feel safe, secure and loved – as it should be for all of us. Bedtime should never be used as a threat – behave or else I'll send you to bed – otherwise children will associate it with naughty behaviour, won't want to go to bed ever, and it will be the beginning of bad sleeping habits which will be very hard to break. It's best to do whatever you can to create good sleeping habits early on. Good habits will improve; bad habits will get worse.

Don't associate bedtime with punishment

First of all, let us dispense with the notion that the later they go to bed, the later they will wake up. This is simply not true. I have always found that the more sleep they have, the more they want. In addition, by this age your toddler will be much more physically active. Hopefully they will be enjoying walks in the park, soaking up the fresh air, spending hours in the sandpit building castles – all an excellent preparation for a good night's sleep. Perhaps they are taking their first social steps into society and joining a little play, gym or music group. With so much to learn, see and discover, a good night's sleep is as invaluable to them as it is to you too. In the same way that tired and grumpy grown-ups do not make for much fun, so tired and grumpy toddlers do not make for good company. So let's start as we mean to go on: with a lot of patience and persistence.

All children's sleep patterns differ, and they have a lot to do with their individual personalities and temperaments. Some children are night owls, preferring to sleep later and rise later; some are early birds, asleep by sunset and awake by sunrise. They are the way they are, and there is nothing we can do to change that. But by establishing a good bedtime routine, you are setting boundaries and teaching them a good lifelong habit. We have already established that a wonderful way to begin winding down to bedtime is with a nice, warm relaxing bath. But as your child moves from being a baby to a toddler, you will find that bath times become much more active affairs.

If they are reluctant to get into the bath, let them take a waterproof toy in with them, or give them an empty washing-up liquid bottle – something of interest to capture their attention. If they are genuinely fearful, perhaps because of a previous bad experience like slipping in the tub or getting soap in their eyes, suggest they bring a favourite teddy or doll and let them give their toy a bath first. Most of the time they will see what fun Teddy is having and will want to jump in with them. (And teddies can always be hung out to drip-dry, or dried with a towel and popped on a radiator.)

You will find that your child will start to stand up in the bath, so it is important that you position a non-slip bath mat securely in place; and always check the water temperature before you pop them into the tub. Try to get the business of washing their body and hair out of the way first so that they can relax and have plenty of time to play. Use only very mild, unperfumed soap and bubble bath, and remember that a lot of novelty soaps and bubble baths contain quite strong detergents and perfumes which can irritate your child if they have sensitive skin. That said, novelty bottles can entice the more fearful toddlers into the bath, so you could always fill them with a more gentle solution if you think it will help things along.

The horrid job of hair-washing should be quick and painless; try not to create a big fuss about it all. I tend only to wash their hair once or twice a week, depending on the state of it – a lot of the time a quick rinse will wash out the remains of dinner! Try to encourage them to lean back while you rinse their hair with a sponge by gently squeezing it from the top of their forehead. You can also use a small plastic cup or container, but I find the shower head is too severe for them. Use a very small amount of gentle shampoo to wash their hair with, and massage it into a big mass of bubbles. Children love bubbles. Add an element of fun by sculpting

silly Mohican hairstyles and shapes out of the bubbles. Show them in the mirror how funny they look – you'll be rewarded with fits of giggles and a demand for more. Rinse by giving them a dry facecloth to cover their eyes in case of soapy suds, and do it as quickly as you can. A lot of the time they fuss briefly, but if they are engrossed in playing with a particular object it soon takes their mind off it.

MISS POPPY'S LIST OF TODDLERS' FAVOURITE BATH TOYS

Waterproof letters and numbers
Toys that float such as ducks or whales
A kitchen colander
A plastic funnel
A small plastic bucket or watering can
Empty plastic bottles, especially washing-up liquid bottles
A bath net which sticks on the side of the bath and holds their toys

Give your child plenty of warning that it's time to get out. If they are absorbed by play, never end it abruptly. Take part instead: suggest rubber ducky gets dry too, or enlist their help in fishing out all the bath toys. My charges have all enjoyed what I call the fishing game. It was invented purely to get a very stubborn little boy I know out of the bath. I give them a fishing net on a pole and they get to fish out all the toys with the net. Great fun indeed. And their favourite bit? Pulling out the plug and watching the water disappear down the drain.

Putting their pyjamas on can sometimes be a bit difficult – they often have a little burst of energy because their mood is happy. If they absolutely refuse to sit still, give them a toy or something to capture their interest while you get on with it. Let them brush their own hair if they want to, and yours too. Show them in the mirror how neat and tidy they look.

Now it's time to brush their teeth. Let them stand at the sink on a little stool or step so that they can reach the bowl. If they have a mirror to look in, so much the better – it's much more fun watching your teeth being brushed than actually doing it. A lot of children tend to swallow instead of spitting out, which is why it is important to try and use only a small amount of toothpaste, and a very gentle type. You can get children's toothpaste in all sorts of tempting flavours (remember to keep it out of reach at all times except for brushing teeth), and there are lots of wonderful novelty toothbrushes available to encourage your child to brush their teeth.

I have invented a very tempting tooth-brushing game to encourage all non-participants.

THE TOOTHBRUSH GAME

Pop a tiny amount of toothpaste on to a soft toothbrush. Entice your child by explaining that you need to clean the house. Gently squeeze their nose, as that's the doorbell, and get them to open up their mouth. Brush upstairs and downstairs, in the room right at the far back corner, in the kitchen at the lower left corner, and don't forget the front teeth that make the front door. Time to gargle, rinse and spit, and then to admire the shiny new house in the mirror. Brushing teeth has never been so much fun.

The time between bath time and bed should be kept as quiet and calm as possible, so no playing any competitive or highly physical games. If a parent comes home from work during this time, it's important they give the child their undivided attention, even if it's just for half an hour. Otherwise you may find them not wanting to go to sleep, or waking up constantly throughout the night just because they want and need to see you. Now is also a good time to offer a last drink of warm milk in a cup, as I always find it helps them to settle.

I am asked all the time about suitable bedtimes. I think that for a child of one to two and a half years, seven o'clock is as good a time as any. I do realise that a lot of parents work very long hours, and that it's hard to come home after a long day at work and not see your little one. But part of loving your child is understanding their needs, and some children just can't make it beyond seven o'clock, especially if their day has been busy and active.

Seven o'clock is a good bedtime

However, you can also alter nap time. If you put it later in the day, they will be prepared to go to bed later; but by later I mean not past eight o'clock. Remember that if your child gets overtired, putting them to bed won't be as easy and they will be more likely to wake up during the night.

Twenty minutes or so before you actually turn the light off is a good time to begin bedtime stories. Let your child choose which books they would like you to read, and find a comfortable place to snuggle down together. I always find it's better to do bedtime stories in their room as they learn to wind down and relax there. It all plays a part in them teaching themselves to go to sleep. Keep bedtime stories gentle – not too many monster or scary-dragon stories – and limit reading time to twenty minutes. You may find yourself coerced into 'just one more', which is fine, so long as it really is just one more. Then it's time to put their sleep suits over

their pyjamas to keep them warm and cosy all night long – and stop them waking up because they are too cold – and pop them into their beds, along with a favourite soft toy, blanket or teddy bear, a big kiss and a cuddle goodnight.

SLEEPLESS NIGHTS

'People who say they sleep like a baby usually don't have one.'
— LEO J. BURKE

Even toddlers from the age of one to two and a half years do not necessarily sleep through the night, but this does not mean that you have to get up and see to them. They learn to put themselves back to sleep if left alone. You will hear sudden yelps or screams on the baby monitor, and although it is important to check on your child, don't rush in and comfort them immediately. Peek in by all means: they may be sitting up, barely awake; they may still be asleep but in strange positions, their bottom up high in the air, or scrunched up into a little ball in the corner like a hedgehog. Unless they are sitting up crying or seem fully awake, working themselves into hysterics, don't go in. Wait to see if they calm down. The majority of the time they go back to sleep in a matter of minutes, or lie there cooing and mumbling to themselves for quite a long while before dropping back off to sleep. They may wake up several times during the night, but they must learn to put themselves back to sleep. If you go in and comfort them during this stage, you will create further sleep problems down the road. Of course, there are times when they need to be physically picked up and comforted – if they are ill, for example, or have had a bad dream. But do not let this turn into a bad habit.

If they cry when being put to bed at night, this is probably caused by separation anxiety – they simply don't want you to go away. You need to offer patience and understanding during this period, but also make them understand that they have to go to bed. This is a crucial time to stand your ground and stop further sleep problems from happening down the road. If you are a working parent, make sure you spend some fun time with your child before you put them to bed. It makes it worse if you come home five minutes before bedtime and then just put them straight down. If the crying starts as soon as you put them to bed, calmly leave the room with the door left slightly open and wait for five minutes. After that enter the room without physically picking them up but stroke them gently and talk to them in a quiet, soothing voice. See if they will lie down in the cot (crib) – most will not but, if they do, gently stroke them to calm them down. Then leave the room again. Wait for another five minutes and then repeat the above procedure. Next time wait ten minutes and repeat the above procedure.

This is the key time to prevent future sleep problems

If your child is in hysterics, pick them up and comfort them in your arms but do not leave the bedroom. Some toddlers have the ability to make themselves physically sick by swallowing huge gulps of air. If you have one of those, you will need to pay extra special attention to their shrieks, and will need to go into their room and reassure them more. When they have calmed down, place them back in their cot (which will be much to their horror) and repeat the above.

Try to remain calm. This is a really hard thing for both of you to go through, but if you tackle it head-on now, it will be much better in the long run. You may find it will take a week of continuing the same procedure, but you must be consistent. If it's too painful for you, enlist the help of your partner or a friend to get through this difficult stage. If your child shares a room with a sibling, then you may have to move them into another room while you get through this stage. Or perhaps you can move your toddler's cot to a corridor

Remain calm and firm

or another room. I've seen cots in bathrooms, corridors and closets, especially in cities where you have to be a bit more creative due to lack of space. If you live in an apartment building you may want to inform your neighbours of your plans, or at least pass along some earplugs!

The most important thing is not to worry: this is not a life-threatening disease, it's just a minor sleep problem and you have made a decision to deal with it. That's half the battle over with before you even begin.

If your problem is that you have an early riser – up with the sun, or even before – then the only thing to do is make sure that they have enough toys or books in their bed to play with in the morning to occupy them for a little while longer. You might want to put a cup of water with a lid on in the bottom of their bed before you go to bed. That way if they wake up thirsty they have something to drink. What you don't want to do it to get into the habit of picking them up at five o'clock in the morning. Encourage them to stay in their beds and occupy themselves as long as they can, even if it's just an extra half an hour. If they share their room with a sibling, however, I'm afraid you'll just have to get up, unless you want the two of them up and about at five in the morning.

MOVING FROM THE COT TO THE BED
The move from the cot to the bed all depends on your child's mobility and climbing skills. I have seen fourteen-month-olds proficient at climbing out of the cot, and two-year-olds still happy to stay put. There is no right age; it really depends on your child. They will begin by throwing toys out of their cot, and then try to retrieve them by attempting to climb out. As soon as you feel they might be in danger of hurting themselves by climbing out, that's the time to make the move.

Moving from a cot to a bed does not have to be a difficult time at all. If your cot's mattress is near the ground, just lower one side of the bars to begin with, and make a nest of pillows for a soft landing should they roll out in the night. If your cot mattress is not so low to the ground, remove the mattress and place it on the floor with one side up against a wall for safety. Larger single mattresses can be used in this way too. Remember to make the new bed enticing and familiar by placing all the same toys and soft animals and blankets that were in the cot on to their new bed for the first two weeks. Let them explore it and jump on it during the daytime so it's not so new and scary at night.

After a week on the floor, the mattress can be moved on to a low bed base. Again, it's best to push one side up against the wall so they only have one side to roll out. Remember to keep a padded nest on the other side to catch night-time fallers. If you prefer, clip-on safety sides can be attached to the open side. They can be found in all good bed shops or department stores. They are easy to assemble, and clip on and off the side of the bed. You may find you have to lie down with them the first two or three nights until they fall asleep; this is fine to start with, but you do not want to turn it into a habit. Oblige for those first few nights, then continue your night-time ritual as before.

The worst times to move your child out of their cot are on the arrival of a new baby, or when you have moved house. The arrival of your new baby might seem to be a natural time to make the *Choose the* transition, but you must remember that your toddler might feel *time* uncomfortable that you have brought a new baby into the house, *carefully* and that they have been kicked out of their bed to make way for them. It is much better to make the move before your new baby arrives, or well after. As far as moving house goes, I have found that it is easier for a child to settle into their new environment with

as many familiar items as possible. Sleep patterns will be disturbed by the stress of the move, so it's not a good idea to add to that by making the cot-to-bed move at this stage. Give them a few weeks to settle into their new location first.

Once your child is sleeping in a bed, it's up to you to decide whether you would prefer to use a duvet or blankets and sheets. The latter do take a bit longer to make in the morning, but they do make it easier to tuck your child in at night, and they tend to stay put on the bed longer. A duvet can be more snug, but it does tend to slip and slide off more easily. You can prevent this by buying a duvet a few sizes larger than you need so that you can tuck it under the mattress. You could also try placing a sheet or throw over the duvet and tucking it under the mattress.

I have found that it usually takes a few days to dawn on them that they can actually get out of the bed freely. Once they do, you may get a little visitor toddling out to see you, or you may hear noises of playtime. If they do keep on wandering out, just keep on popping them back into their bed. Be patient and persistent. There will be times when they are not feeling well, or have suffered an emotional upset; on these occasions they should be greeted with open

arms and a cuddle. You know your child best, and it's up to you
to distinguish between the genuine and the Oscar-winning
performances. If you do start to have tears and tantrums, comfort
them at first but then be firm: pop them back into their bed and
pull the bedroom door almost shut, keeping it a tiny bit open
using a doorstop. If a tug of war begins with the door, you have to
stand your ground and hold on firmly. Let them see that you are
safely there at the other side of the door, but make sure it's not
open enough for them to squeeze out. Calmly tell them that it is
time to go back to bed. Let them carry on for a maximum of five
minutes, then enter the room calmly and pick them up, comfort
them and place them back into their bed. Repeat this procedure
and extend the time you allow them to scream and shout from five
minutes to ten minutes. I know it's painful and emotionally
exhausting, but you really want to nip this in the bud here and *Don't give in*
now. If you give in and let them stay up it will be harder and harder
to get them to bed. Usually by the third time of holding the door
they get so exhausted that the next time you pop them back into
their beds they will stay there. It will help if you stay with them for
a little while, just to comfort them and calm them down so that
they are able to fall asleep peacefully. Once you've got them to
sleep, you can be proud of yourself: it is not an easy thing to deal
with. But you must be persistent, and if they repeat the same
behaviour you must act accordingly again and again. It will end
when they see they have no leverage with you. Remember to keep
calm. It's just a passing stage.

If you hear them getting out of bed and playing with their toys,
the best course of action is to go back into the room and explain
that playtime is over, pop them back into their bed and let them
keep the toys they were playing with at the bottom of the bed or
next to them (just so long as they have no sharp edges or tiny
pieces that look like they could be swallowed). If they continue to

get out of the bed, remove the toys from their reach by putting them away in a toy box or cupboard, safely out of sight. And if tears and tantrums follow, repeat the above procedure of returning them to their beds. Don't expect perfection at first; change takes time and commitment. You must be fair but firm.

ILLNESS

'When I was sick and lay a-bed,
I had two pillows at my head,
And all my toys beside me lay,
To keep me happy all the day.'
– *The Land of Counterpane,* ROBERT LOUIS STEVENSON

There are certain signs to look for to alert you to the fact that your child is not feeling well. You will probably notice a change in their everyday temperament and behaviour. They just won't seem themselves at all – they may be grumpy or fractious, cry more and have no energy, or simply want to sleep more during the day. They may be non-cooperative and difficult, and they may lose their appetite. Your toddler is only human, and you have to expect a certain amount of disrupted night-time sleep when they are feeling unwell. Often sleepless nights occur leading up to an illness – the symptoms may not have fully arrived but your child will be feeling under the weather and not themselves.

The symptoms may be more obvious, of course – a cough, for example, or a runny nose. You should also keep an eye on your child's temperature. Normal body temperature is 37°C or 98.4°F. A temperature higher than 37.5°C or 99.5°F is considered a fever and should be treated with Calpol to reduce it as quickly as possible. Temperatures higher than 39°C or 103°F should be immediately reported to a doctor. I have found the easiest and quickest way to take the temperature of a child over the age of two is with an ear thermometer. They are very easy to use – just place it in the ear for a few seconds, press a button and it quickly displays an accurate temperature. Children can even do it by themselves. For younger children, use a press-on thermometer which you place upon their forehead for an accurate reading.

If your child is reluctant to take medicine, offer a pill hidden in a spoon of ice cream or their favourite yogurt. Liquid medicine is usually easier to administer, and children's medicines come in a variety of flavours, although you should offer a drink straight after they have taken the medicine to wash away any residual taste in their mouth. Keep a written note of the time and amount of medicine given, along with a note of their temperature, so that you have a clear record to present to your doctor if need be.

If your child has a fever, make sure they are not overdressed. If the fever is very high, remove all their outer clothes down to their underwear or nappy. Sponge them down with tepid water to reduce very high fevers and offer them lots of cold water to sip. High fevers can dehydrate your child quickly, so it's imperative you feed them as many fluids as they will take. (Some doctors suggest offering a small amount of a fizzy drink heavily diluted with water, as the sugar will help them rehydrate more quickly.) When putting them to bed, only use a sheet to cover them – no heavy blankets – and make sure their bedroom is not overheated.

If a high fever is accompanied by vomiting, rashes, headaches or stiffness, you must contact your doctor's surgery immediately. For body rashes accompanied by a high fever, do the glass test: if you roll a glass over the rash and it fades away to nothing, it's safe; if not, consult your doctor immediately as it could be a sign of meningitis. Most GPs and paediatricians are used to a constant stream of worried and anxious calls from parents and care-givers, so do not feel afraid to call and voice your worries and concerns. In my experience, a mother's instinct about her own child is always spot on.

Untreated, high fevers can become very distressing. Your child can go all stiff and convulse into spasms. If this happens, you must make sure that they are placed on their side so that they don't choke on their own saliva, and insert the back of a rounded spoon into their mouth to prevent them from biting their tongue. They must be taken to hospital immediately for closer examination.

The common cold can be really unpleasant for your child, but you can help them feel more comfortable by keeping a bowl of hot water in the room – preferably near the radiator – into which you have dropped a little natural decongestant oil such as Olbas Oil. You can also sprinkle one or two drops on to their sheets to help their breathing throughout the night, or drape a wet towel sprinkled with a few drops over a radiator. If their throat is sore and red, offer them a drink of warm water with lemon and honey to soothe it. Ice lollies are also soothing on their throat.

A cold may be connected to an ear infection. If your child is constantly rubbing or pulling at their ear and it is red or swollen, this is usually a sign of an irritation or infection. They may squeal as they lay their head down because their ear hurts. If you suspect an ear infection, you should consult your doctor. Make sure your child's ears are dry after swimming or hair-washing by wafting a hairdryer over each ear for a few seconds to prevent a build-up of water.

If a cold is accompanied by a hacking dry cough that wakes them in the night, take them into the bathroom and switch on the hot water tap or the shower to create steam. This will help your child to breath. Try to keep them calm by comforting them and rubbing their back. If the coughing continues to affect your child's breathing, you should consult your doctor.

Vomiting bugs can really frighten your child, so you need to be kind, understanding and very patient with them during this unpleasant stage. Place a bucket or bowl near their bed, just in case they feel they can catch it in time. Change their clothes and sheets as quickly as you can and without fuss. Sprinkle a few drops of lavender oil on the mattress cover before you replace the sheets, to help take the nasty smell away. Offer them constant sips of ice-cold water – no gulping, or the vomiting will be encouraged. Never offer milk or dairy products when they have a stomach upset as they are too rich to digest. Stick to plain toast, salted crackers and boiled rice to line their stomachs until the vomiting stops. Keep hot and cold foods separate, as mixing them could cause further vomiting. As always, consult your doctor's office immediately if the vomiting is associated with a high fever.

Once children start attending a playgroup or preschool, the number of germs they are exposed to multiplies. It may seem as though they have a new cold or runny nose every single week. All you can do at this stage is to offer them plenty of fresh fruit and vegetables, help

them to remember to wash their hands and make sure they drink enough water – these will all help to build up their immune system.

When a child is feeling ill you need to be a little bit more flexible and try to make them feel as cherished and as comfortable as possible. Make them a little bed on the sofa with a pillow and a blanket or quilt. Make a special activity box and fill it with some new reading books, colouring pens, arts and crafts materials and maybe a simple board game like snakes and ladders – whatever you think they will enjoy. Keep it for special not-feeling-well days only, and leave it near your sick patient so they can play should they feel up to it.

Don't worry about the routine

Do not worry if your routine goes out of the window, but do encourage naps as much as possible. Cuddle down with them on the sofa, read a story together and hopefully they will drop off for a while. The more sleep, the better. Bed times may be later, but try as much as you can to stick to your regular time, and be prepared for night-time disturbances. All you can do is offer comfort and cuddles in the middle of the night, check temperatures and administer medicines. Make sure they are comfortable and dry, give them a fresh drink of water and try to get them relaxed enough to go back to sleep – even if you do have to fall asleep with them lying in your lap. In times of need, you just need to do whatever you can.

COMMON AILMENTS

If you are worried about your child, you should always contact your doctor. But there are some common ailments that you can diagnose and treat at home.

TUMMY ACHE

Tummy ache is often the result of either constipation or wind (gas). Press your fingers on to your child's tummy. If it hurts them, it's wind; if the tummy is hard, it's constipation. Offer apple juice with a tablespoon of prune juice combined to ease constipation. Wind can be flushed out by positioning your baby over your shoulder or across your lap and rubbing their back in a circular motion. A bottle of cooled, boiled water can also help.

Natural yogurt works wonders for tummy upsets of all kinds. If the pain continues and spreads down from their side, contact your doctor.

CUTS AND SCRAPES
Place pressure on the cut or scrape to stop the bleeding, and wash with warm water and soap. Apply an antiseptic or a natural tea-tree ointment and cover with a non-stick dressing.

BUMPS AND BRUISES
Place ice on to the affected area to reduce the swelling. Bruises clear much more quickly with the aid of arnica cream rubbed directly on to the bruised area as soon as possible.

SPLINTERS
Splinters tend to make their own way out if soaked in warm salt water and nudged out with a pair of fine-tipped tweezers.

BANGS TO THE HEAD
Bangs to the head must be treated with caution. Apply pressure if there is any bleeding, and an ice pack to reduce swelling. But you must look for any other signs accompanying the bang. If there is any vomiting, headaches, nosebleeds, earache or drowsiness, you should go to casualty immediately. Any head injury to a child under the age of one year should immediately be reported to your doctor, or the child taken to hospital.

BURNS

Hold the burn under cool running water for eight to ten minutes. Apply antiseptic cream and a non-stick dressing. Sunburn can be treated with aloe vera gel, and if your child is affected by sunburn, they should be given plenty of liquids to prevent dehydration which can lead to sunstroke.

CHOKING

If you suspect that a child under the age of one is choking, lift both their arms up in the air to open the airways. If they are unable to cough it up, place them upside down, face down on your lap and give them a good pat on the upper back, between the shoulders. Repeat if the food is still stuck. Always call for medical assistance if your baby stops breathing. Cuddle, comfort and reassure afterwards.

For a child over the age of one, you must use the Heimlich manoeuvre. Quickly get behind the child and wrap your arms around their waist. Clench one hand into a tight fist, leaving your thumb out. With pressure from your other hand force the fist in the child's midline just above the navel but below the ribs. Press your fist into the child's abdomen with quick inwards and upwards thrusts. It may take several thrusts to dislodge the food or cause of obstruction. A child who can cough may lift both arms up high to help open the airways.

POTTY-TRAINING

'Never hurry and never worry.'
– Charlotte's Web, E. B. WHITE

Potty-training used to be looked upon quite differently to the way it is today, no doubt because an absence of washing machines, hot water and disposable nappies meant that mothers were keen to get their children to use the potty as soon as possible. My experience with children, however, has led me to believe that it's no use potty-training your child until they are fully aware of their own bodily functions. This generally happens around the age of eighteen months; it is only then that they become aware of urination as a voluntary action rather than a reflex one – but you still only have about a second to catch it as it usually happens there and then! Potty-training before the age of eighteen months is called conditioning: the child is unaware of the sensation to pee, and just does it automatically when the nappy is removed and their bottom is placed on a cold-rimmed potty. Don't let family or friends pressure you into starting potty-training before your child is ready. It makes much more sense if they are actually aware of the sensation of needing to go before you start; they will be more cooperative and better able to learn and understand the full potty-training process.

Now more than ever it is important to remember never to compare your child with others. You have a unique, individual child who was born with a temperament and personality that you are patiently nurturing. There are no right and wrong ages for them *Choose a good* to develop, just guidelines that you can follow. All you can do is *time to start* teach and assist them, and trust that they will accomplish what *potty training* they need to in their own time. The time you choose to begin potty-training should be as stress-free as possible, more for your sake than your child's. If a new baby has recently been introduced to the family, it's probably better to wait a month or so as your toddler will be psychologically adjusting and not quite ready for more changes just yet. Potty-training can be more convenient if begun during the summer months because your child will be wearing fewer clothes and able to run around nappy-free in the great outdoors. But don't worry if that is not possible: the important thing is to know and feel when your child is ready.

To begin with you will need a plastic potty. There are many different types, but I find the simpler they are, the better. I prefer the ones that are brightly coloured, light to carry and easy to clean; but you can also buy potties with novelty faces on them, which seem to be very popular with two-year-olds, and even some that burst into song with the deed is done!

At around eighteen months they will start to tell you they need changing when they are wet – some toddlers even remove their own wet nappy. If you watch them closely you will also notice their facial expressions when they are peeing; all of a sudden they become aware of the sensation. This is a good time to begin introducing the potty. I normally do it first just before bath time. I don't know if it's the sound of rushing water filling up the bath that makes them want to go, or maybe that they have a habit of doing it when they take off their nappy, but if you are lucky during those first few attempts you might just catch one in the potty. It will be greeted with huge curiosity, and their achievement should be rewarded with great praise. Mostly, though, the first few times they sit on the potty they won't do much, and they won't stay there for very long. They will enjoy the novelty, however, and will undoubtedly want to examine the potty inside and out. By all means encourage them. You could even sit Teddy or their favourite toy on the potty so that they understand what it is for. Indeed, I sometimes use a toy as a companion for them all the way through the potty-training process. Teddy gets to wear a nappy, practise sitting on the loo, and he even gets new underwear to practise keeping dry. It seems to relieve some of the pressure toddlers can feel during potty-training, and can be a comfort to them during the times when they feel disappointed or upset – especially when they have wet their new underwear.

You should never force a child to sit on the potty or else you are in for difficult times ahead. But if they are reluctant, you could try cutting a hole in one of their nappies and placing it on the potty. This will make them feel more safe and comfortable and help to associate the potty with the nappy – and what you do in it! I like to try and make potty time fun by keeping a special audio tape of *Make potty* songs or nursery rhymes specifically for listening to while they are *time fun* sitting on the potty. You'll be amazed at how many songs and rhymes can be learned during this time. Keep a special story book and only read it at potty time. It all adds a little extra incentive for them to look forward to potty time rather than dread it.

The next thing to do is to introduce the potty straight after meal times, morning, noon and night. Place it somewhere warm and comfortable, and get down on the floor next to your child so that you are at the same level. You could hold their hands for reassurance, and read a book or sing a song together – anything to help them relax and feel comfortable. To start with they will only sit on the potty for a few minutes at a time, and you should never force them to remain sitting. Some children like to stand up and down checking to see if anything is there, and it's the funniest thing when they do actually do something – the look of shock and delight on their faces! I knew one little boy who burst into tears when I flushed his first major bowel movement down the loo. He demanded it back immediately in order to save it to show his parents how clever he had been. They were in fact both away on business at the time, so we compromised by calling them up on the telephone to tell them the great news. They responded with sheer delight and lots of praise, telling all their business associates who were sitting around the conference table. I fear the non-parents among them must have thought they were completely nuts! But it did the trick, and I learned to empty the potty without him seeing from then on.

Young children do find the mechanics of flushing toilets quite fascinating, but a bit scary too. I think that maybe they worry that they will be washed away down the bowl with the gushing water, so I do try to familiarise them with toilets by letting them come along to the loo with me and allowing them to flush and see that I am not washed away. Now is also a good time to teach good hygiene habits by showing them how you always wash your hands after going to the loo. Children are always more than happy to play with water, so make sure they have easy access to the sink by placing a stool or steps there, and provide them with soap (which, if you don't supervise them, will be used in one wash). Make sure that your hot water tap is set at a low temperature so that you don't scald eager hand-washers. I like to give them their own special little towel, and they can be responsible for putting it in the washing machine on wash day, and can even hang it out to dry. Never forget you have an eager little helper who actually enjoys stuffing washing in the washing machine, putting in the soap powder and pressing the magic buttons.

Teach hand-washing now

After they have performed on the potty you must always express your delight and tell them what a big girl or boy they are. Never be cross or show disapproval at an empty potty, just try again next time. If they demand the potty twelve times a day and still nothing happens, they might be rather enjoying all the fuss they are creating, and too much time on the potty can have an adverse reaction. Try to keep it for after meals, when you are just about to leave the house and when you come back home from an outing.

If they really show no interest in the potty, invite a friend over with an older child who will quite happily sit on their potty and perform. This usually encourages younger children to want to copy their behaviour. If there is still no interest, take the potty away for a week or two and then start afresh.

Once you are getting results in the potty, you can let your child put on their big-boy or big-girl underwear, even if it is only for a few hours a day. Try to have a bit of underwear time every day, and increase it as each day passes. If you are out and about and do not want to lug the potty with you, always be prepared for accidents with a change of clothes, fresh underwear, a dry nappy and a plastic bag to put the wet clothes in. After two weeks of practising you can try going the whole day in underpants. Prepare yourself with lots of dry ones and some extra clothes, and pay close attention to your child. Watch for sudden grasps, leaps and wriggling movements, which are clues that they need to go. Move in quickly with a potty. One clean day will lead to another as their confidence grows.

When your child is comfortable on the potty – which will normally be after the age of two – you can introduce them to the grown-up toilet. Fix a child's seat to the bowl, as most grown-up loos are too big for them. Children's toilet seats can be easily found in all department shops and baby-care shops. Place a stool or some steps next to the toilet so that they can climb up by themselves and have a foot rest. An old wooden box works wonders too. Stay with them to start with, holding their hands or reading a book together to offer reassurance. If they keep getting up and down from the toilet, simply stop paying attention to them and don't read the book until they stay sitting. Don't expect them to sit for too long on the toilet, but do encourage them to go to the bathroom by telling them that's where you do your pee and poo.

Introduce the grown-up toilet after the age of two

Peeing and pooing are two very different things to your child. They will be more than happy to pee in the potty or the grown-up toilet, but pooing without the safety of their padded nappy is a different story. I don't quite know why this should be so, but you can encourage them by allowing them to see you doing it on the loo (did I mention that when you become a parent all privacy goes out of the window?). And you must be patient and not allow yourself to get upset when they dirty their underwear or nappy, or at least don't let them see that you are upset about it. Explain when you are changing them that next time if they want to be big they could try doing it on the loo or the potty.

If you know when your child's bowel movements are likely to be, say after breakfast or dinner, aim for a potty or toilet period at that exact moment. But never force them or make a fuss if nothing happens, just try again tomorrow. Boys benefit by watching their fathers or brothers going to the loo standing up, and they soon realise what tricks they can get up to. You can even buy things called toilet-training targets – plastic floating toys to go in your toilet bowl for little boys to aim at. I've seen them used in quite a few American households with some success – boys do seem to respond to this method, so you could always try popping a ping-pong ball in the bowl if you can't find anything else. Remember to warn any visitors before they go! Also, keep an eye out for any younger siblings taking an interest and trying to fish them out. You can buy safety catches for the toilet seat so that they can't lift up the lid.

It is a good idea to get your child used to visiting bathrooms outside of the home, so if you are visiting friends, let your toddler come to their bathroom with you so that they can see it is safe and friendly. When in a restaurant or shop, take them to the loo and use it yourself first, then see if they would like to try after you. If they would, hold their hands for comfort and stay in the cubicle with them. Wash your hands together afterwards, even if it's only you that has been – and remember that automatic drying machines are always a good source of entertainment.

Sleeping through the night without a nappy may be a slower process for your child than learning to be dry during the day. A good time to start is with nap time. Two hours is a good amount of time for them to get used to the idea of falling asleep without the safety and security of their nappy, and a good stepping stone to dry nights. Put them on the potty before nap time, and then pop them down for a sleep without their nappy. If they are dry afterwards, praise them and tell them what a big boy or girl they are. Give them a nice refreshing drink and try sitting them on the potty again. Don't rush the process of sleeping though the night without a nappy, though. Lots of children between the age of three and four are still sleeping with a nappy on at night-time. Check the nappy in the morning and see how damp it is. If it's very damp, there is no way they are ready to start sleeping without one. If it is dry, or only slightly wet, you can begin. Prepare the bed with a waterproof mattress cover, and sprinkle the sheets with a few drops of lavender oil for a calm, soothing smell. Keep a clean pair of sheets handy in the bedroom for middle-of-the-night accidents. Night lights and landing lights should be left on to lead the way safely to the bathroom in the night. To start with, go into your child's room last thing at night before you go to bed and carry them to the loo. Then pop them back into bed all snug and cosy. I'm not a big advocate of continuing this for too long, as it will become habit-forming, and really you want your child to wake up when they feel the sensation of wanting to go to the loo. But it is OK for a couple of weeks, and it will reduce the amount of laundry you have to do.

If your child wakes up wet, just bathe and change them without making a fuss and try again the next night. If you feel after one week you are making no progress, just pop a nappy back on and try again in a couple of weeks' time. There might be times when you feel you are regressing rather than progressing. These could be times when your child feels under the weather or is overexcited by thoughts of Christmas or an impending birthday. It may be things you are not even aware of – starting a playgroup or a simple scare like a fall in the playground or a barking dog – anything that may have caused anxiety or excitement.

Your child's diet also plays a big part in potty-training. Remember that you should always offer them plenty of liquids, fresh fruit and vegetables. Stay away from processed foods which contain large amounts of salts and sugar, as do crisps, sweets and biscuits – they can all cause constipation, and that will set your child back during this crucial time. Constipation can be a painful experience for your child, but you can prevent it by offering plenty of roughage in their daily diet – oat cereals, brown rice, dried fruits with the skin intact – and water, water and more water. Prune juice works wonders in minutes: blend it into a smoothie with crushed ice if your child refuses to drink it.

Expect setbacks, and remember the more laid-back you are about it, the easier time you will both have.

TANTRUMS AND TIARAS

'Love me when I least deserve it,
because that's when I really need it.'
– SWEDISH PROVERB

Toddlers are perfectly delightful, full to the brim with curiosity and eager to explore anything and everything. They will turn over every fallen leaf and empty every cupboard to see what treasures they might discover. What will it look like? What will it taste like? What will it sound like when I drop it or shake it? At this age it's not naughtiness, it's learning and discovering. Tipping over dirty nappy buckets, emptying your purse, smothering your expensive new face cream all over the carpet floor – these are all their way of figuring out the world in which they live. I find that the most intelligent children are the ones who are into absolutely everything; as exhausting as it may be, it is a necessary part of their learning and growth.

So you have a toddler with an abundance of energy and curiosity. The problem is that they are incapable of understanding formal methods of discipline. They are not being naughty anyway, and it will do more harm than good at this stage if you tell a child off when they have no understanding of the difference between right and wrong behaviour. It will lead to increased insecurity and mega tantrums at a later age.

By the age of fifteen months your child will start to test their boundaries and limits in order to feel safe and secure. I worked for a wonderful family of four children whose limits and boundaries *Boundaries* were vague and misconstrued. They did not really know what *are essential* they were allowed to do and what they weren't. This led to the children being very insecure, suffering behavioural and learning problems and becoming unpopular at school, where they were always in trouble. The bottom line was that they were miserable, and their parents could not quite figure out why. After all, they gave their children everything they asked for and let them do whatever they wanted.

It was obvious to me, as an outsider, that the children never knew where they stood. They were confused about how far they could go with others, and were often unaware that their behaviour caused others to flinch, run for cover or even scream for help. Fortunately, their parents were smart enough to seek professional help, and they all began the slow process of reconditioning as a family group. Boundaries were set: a fixed time for bed, the children were distracted and prevented from hitting others, whining fits and temper tantrums were not given in to. The process taught the children that they were being cared for, and that the parents knew what was best for them. The children started to feel secure, and their behaviour improved beyond measure.

Your toddler will almost certainly go through what I call the diva stage, and you can expect movie-star behaviour and demands: they want you to help build a tower block with them, but the first piece you touch is the wrong one and is greeted with bellowing shrieks of disapproval. Children of this age do not have the vocabulary to explain exactly what it is they want or need. Most of the time they don't even know what it is they want. It is a transitional time for them, halfway between being a baby and a child, and it can be scary for them. They want to show their independence, but they also fear losing you. They will learn every button to press in order to get a reaction from you. If you react and create and shout, they will press that button for a second, third and fourth performance. And let's face it: one drama queen in the family is quite enough, thank you.

Take control

This is not a good time to offer a wide selection of choices, as this will just add to their insecurity. You need to be assertive and decisive by taking control of the situation and keeping options to a minimum. I once observed a little lad of about twenty months lying on the floor in fits of tears at an ice-cream shop while his confused father kept on reeling off the names of the flavours of ice cream available. 'Straciatelli with chocolate chips, Straciatelli without chocolate chips, green-tea infusion with lemon verbena, green-tea infusion without lemon verbena …' The poor father was as confused as his son as to why he was reacting in the way he was. I tried to help by suggesting he pick the little chap off the floor and we go outside the shop for a cuddle and calm down. This of course caused more screaming as he thought he was not getting any ice cream at all, but once he had calmed down in his father's arms I asked him what colour liked. 'Red,' he piped up clearly, so I went into the shop and bought a strawberry ice cream which was greeted with a big smile. No fuss, no complicated decision-making – I gave him a clear, simple choice.

To help a child make their own choices, always keep it simple and make sure it is clear what you are offering. Don't offer choices about things that are going to happen in the future, as toddlers live in the exact moment. When getting ready to leave for a trip to the park, ask: 'Would you like to go to the park in your buggy, or would you like to walk?' 'What would you like to bring to play with, your ball or your bucket and spade?' 'Would you like a piece of cheese or an apple for a snack?' Simple decision-making without overloading them with choices helps them to feel in control and therefore less frustrated and more independent.

Little things that may seem silly to you can be of huge importance to a toddler, and you must choose your battles carefully. If there is an alternative solution – a white-bread sandwich instead of a brown one – it's best just to go with the flow to keep the peace. This does not mean that you are giving in to their every whim, just that you are listening to their reasonable requests and allowing them to *Give in to* make small decisions for themselves. Just be sensible about it: *some requests* if your child requests six different types of cereal for breakfast, maybe just this once sprinkle six different varieties into their bowl – but be careful to put four of the boxes of cereal out of sight so that the following morning you only have two types to choose from. That way they will feel happier and more independent, and you will have managed the situation wonderfully by not having to say no all the time, which is like waving a red rag to a bull at this age.

Try to answer their requests optimistically, otherwise you will find a whole day may have passed you by and the only communication you have had will have been negative: 'Don't touch that, don't do that, no, no and no again.' Try to offer alternative suggestions: 'We won't play with my brand-new computer, but let's play with water and make bubbles in the sink.' Be enthusiastic and you will find the sudden screams turn to giggles of excitement. When you are dealing with children of this age you need to become a master of the art of creative distraction.

This is not to say that they don't need to understand what the word 'no' means, or that certain behaviour is unacceptable; just that you need to learn how to divert their attention as much as you are able. Prevention is better than cure! One very precious eighteen-month-old girl I knew went through a stage of not wanting to sit in her buggy. She would arch her body into a stiff plank, which was virtually impossible to bend into the seat of the buggy. To start with I just used to tickle her and she would crumple easily into her seat, but that only worked for a few days before she got wise to it. I suggested she be allowed to bring along a toy pet, and I produced a ball of string to act as a leash. She immediately went to fetch her stuffed hedgehog. We tied some string around its neck and she happily leaped into her pushchair, dragging the hedgehog behind her. We even had to stop for a drink of water for it. By inventing that little game we avoided a massive confrontation that would have only ended up making us all feel bad.

Ignore them when they are having a tantrum

There are, of course, times when there is absolutely nothing you can do but let them get on with a tantrum. The best way to cope with this is to ignore it: don't respond, don't communicate, just look away and, if you can, walk into another room and get on with something else. If they follow you or are holding on to your legs and won't let go, pretend they are not there. It will obviously infuriate them, but they will eventually learn that this kind of behaviour receives no attention from you whatsoever. Some children hold their breath until they are blue in the face. If so, stand in front of them holding both their arms and blow directly into their mouth, which will make them catch their breath. If they won't open their mouth, tickle them under their arms – that normally does the trick. Don't forget to comfort them afterwards, as it's just as scary for them as it is for you. Children do actually frighten themselves during a tantrum (as well as you and half the neighbourhood). If you feel your child is liable to cause themselves physical harm during a tantrum, hold on to them tightly until they calm down. Sometimes blowing gently on them and talking in a calm, soothing voice helps.

Tantrums are a natural part of growing up, but they can be exacerbated by tiredness, sickness, sheer boredom, excess energy or the arrival of a new baby in the house. Any form of change or stress your child is unable to understand can result in a tantrum. Sometimes too much information too soon can stressful for a child. I watched one little boy suffer terribly with tantrums due to the fact that he was a brilliant little Lego builder. His parents invested in complicated Lego structures more suited to a twelve-year-old than a three-year-old. He was able to put them together, but unable to understand that they were more ornamental than play-proof, and as soon as he tried to play his rough-and-tumble games with them, they fell apart – and so did he. They exceeded his limitations, and this was cause for great frustration. Toddlers need boundaries, and they need you to understand their limits.

Tantrums can also be caused by separation anxiety – just plain old fear of being separated from you. Leaving a child at any point during the ages of one to two and a half years is not an easy process for either of you. That's why it is a good idea to expose your child to as many other adults, children and social environments as possible from an early age. They will begin to learn to feel safe in other places apart from home, and in the company of people other than you. Gradually they will build relationships with your friends, neighbours or their grandparents so that if you ever have to leave them, you can do so in a familiar environment. If you do leave your child in unfamiliar surroundings, let them bring a toy, teddy or favourite blanket, something that smells and reminds them of home. Familiar drinking cups, bibs and spoons can also help if they are eating away from home, as can their favourite foods. Feeding time at home is always a good moment for you to make an exit, as they are busy eating. In unfamiliar places you should stay with your child for a short while to help them settle in and find an interesting toy to capture their interest. If possible, let the person who is caring for them initiate the play and, once they seem slightly captivated, make your exit. You can explain to an older child of two and a half years that you are leaving and will be back shortly, but be prepared for tears – it is a completely normal reaction. The best response is just to leave and let the carer look after them. Give it fifteen minutes and then call on the telephone

Introduce your child to other environments

to see if they have calmed down. Most of the time you will be assured that they are perfectly alright. And then, of course, you will feel unwanted!

Saying no to a one-year-old can cause them to burst into tears of absolute shock. They are hurt by the change in your voice and tone. The power of your voice and your body language are very powerful means of sending messages of approval and disapproval to a young child. This is how they will begin to learn the difference between right and wrong behaviour. As I have said before, they are not able to understand clearly before the age of two years what it is that they have done wrong, but this does not mean that you should never say no to them. Of course you should, and when you do it you should get down to their level, look directly into their eyes and say no in a deep, resonant voice. Then physically move away from them showing your disapproval. You may or may not be greeted with tears or shrieks of indignant belief; but be comforted by the fact that you are setting a boundary which will ultimately make them feel safe and secure.

Look directly at them when saying 'no'

Learning how to get along with others is part of growing up, and a certain standard of social behaviour is expected. However, with children of this age you can throw all your expectations of immaculate behaviour straight out of the window. I have met eighteen-month-old barbarians who have attempted to drag newfound friends around by the hair, and it is always such a shock to parents when their normally gorgeously behaved little Johnny suddenly turns out to be capable of grievous bodily harm. If this happens to you, don't worry! Believe it or not, it is all perfectly natural behaviour, and it certainly doesn't mean you shouldn't expose your child to other toddlers – in fact the sooner you do so, the better. Increase their social interaction by taking them to the park or playground to observe others at play. This is also a great way for them to run off some of that excess energy, which can manifest itself in a number of ways, including hitting, biting, breaking things and throwing physically demanding tantrums. In the case of hitting or biting, always observe your child closely and watch for escalating trouble spots. If they are happily playing with their tricycle and another child arrives thinking they might like to have a go, you know you are in for trouble. The best thing to do is to intervene – try to bring in another interesting toy or car to zoom around in as an alternative. Offer it to either child, as they really do not understand the concept of taking turns at this point, and trying to remove either of them from the tricycle will just be a cause for tears. If hitting or biting has already taken place, you need to remove the culprit immediately. Say no as firmly as you can, trying not to make too big a thing of it, then move on and try to distract them with something else to play with. I'm afraid that the more attention you give bad behaviour at this age, the more it will happen.

Of course, there are toddlers who develop more worrying behavioural difficulties. Because toddlers' behaviour is so erratic, however, it can be difficult to distinguish between what is normal and what needs professional attention. In my experience, worryingly bad behaviour in toddlers often stems from neglect. Children who are endlessly having tantrums, destroy personal property as a matter of course and are extremely violent towards others, especially siblings, tend to be reacting to their environment. Frequently these children are diagnosed with learning and behavioural problems. Sometimes these diagnoses are valid; but often I find that the symptoms can be treated by good basic care and attention from a well-balanced, kind, understanding, non-reactive adult.

If, however, the problems do not resolve themselves through consistent parenting skills, and if the toddler is constantly angry, violent and unmanageable without moments of joy, laughter and fun, it may be that there is a behavioural problem. If you are at all worried, you should talk to your doctor who can refer you to a specialist in child psychology. They will be able to shine some light on your child's behaviour and suggest ways in which it can be resolved. Don't be afraid to ask for help. Behavioural difficulties can be treated, and the more you know about them, the more you will be able to help your child grow up happy and healthy.

ENERGETIC, FUN-LOVING BUT FIRM MARY POPPINS MENTOR URGENTLY SOUGHT FOR JAMES, AGED TWO. SINGLE-PARENT FAMILY. GRANNY FLAT AND CAR PROVIDED.

What the advertisement forget to mention was that the granny flat came complete with its own granny!

James was an extremely bouncy boy with a loving, hard-working mum; the grandmother had been his main carer until I arrived. Granny was a delight, but full to the brim of 1950s parenting ideals and still of the belief that children should be seen and not heard. She was also in her late seventies which meant that, as wonderfully kind and nurturing as she was, she was physically unable to cope with an extremely energetic young boy. As a result, James had become quite a handful: he was uncooperative, negative and had taken to screaming at the top of his voice, mostly because of his unmet needs. I think he was bored, suffered from a lack of stimulation and was clearly not getting enough physical exercise – there just did not seem to be a lot of fun in his life. He always seemed to be in trouble with his granny, who really did not understand that what he was displaying at that age was not naughtiness but curiosity and excess energy.

James spent the majority of his time inside the house being told not to jump on the sofa and not to make a mess. His only trips out were to the supermarket or to visit his granny's friends – even those had petered out because Granny could no longer control his behaviour and her friends had requested the visits stop. So all in all everyone was feeling quite frustrated with each other, and it was no wonder that he was a handful.

My first task was to introduce James to other adults and children, and the best way of doing this was to take him to the local playground and park. There he could meet and mix with other children of his own age, run and jump to get rid of some of that excess energy, and explore without getting into trouble. That way, James would become more used to being around others and therefore more comfortable and relaxed in their presence. The problem was that James absolutely refused to leave the house. He was at that stage where he said 'no' to everything, clearly enjoying the attention the negativity caused, no doubt due to the fact he was bored. Moreover, he had only ever been driven places; the mere mention of a walk brought shrieks of horror! So it was key that I turned it all into some sort of game. I suggested we take Teddy or one of his favourite toys on an adventure, which immediately captured his attention. He went and found an action figure of some sort and we popped him into the buggy. I told James he was going to have to push, and immediately saw a twinkle in his eyes.

First, however, we needed something for us to have a picnic at the park. I let James choose snacks for his action figure while I packed a few fish-shaped crackers, a box of raisins, a few slices of cheese, breadsticks and some apple juice. I then found an empty pot, washed it out and filled it up with water for James and his action figure. It was just the right size to fit into James's pocket, and he was very chuffed to have his own water bottle with a screw-top lid. I think it made him feel very grown-up indeed. I also suggested he take his bucket and spade, which were neatly packed away and only used on summer holidays. Soon enough, what had previously been a battleground had turned into an adventure, with James eager to participate. Off we set at a snail's pace, with James pushing the buggy and stopping every three seconds to take a sip of water from his very own bottle. It didn't matter: we had all afternoon to wander and it was important that I let James take his time and go at his own speed.

The walking was a bit of a novelty at first, but I was hardly prepared for what happened next. I was holding James's hand as we were crossing a main road when, in the blink of an eye, he stuck out his other hand and hailed a black cab to an abrupt halt. I stood there with my mouth open and was about to explain to the taxi driver that we did not need his services when James began to scream like a banshee. The taxi driver jumped out of his cab and opened the passenger door for James. As he climbed in, the screeching stopped. The driver took one look at my face and said, 'You win some, you lose some, love. It ain't worth the fight!' Suddenly I found myself sitting in the back of the taxi, astonished by this little boy's streetwise knowledge, and wondering how on earth a two-year-old had just managed to get the better of me!

Next time I was a little more innovative. Before we set off on our walk to the park I collected up a couple of his toy cars – a tractor and a black cab – and with great patience I let James push the cars along the ground until we reached the entrance to the park (which was, I might add, a mere ten-minute walk from the house). James loved this and was quite happy marching along at two miles per hour, one hand holding on to the buggy, the other running his tractor over the surface of any wall or building he could find. When he asked, I popped him into his buggy, but I encouraged him to walk whenever I could.

As time went on, he preferred to stand on the back bar of the buggy and put all his sand toys on the seat. I think it somehow made him feel cool! Our walks gradually became gathering times: he collected sticks, rocks, leaves and anything else that captured his interest. We shoved it all into the bottom of the buggy and took it home for close examination and much discussion. Many of the larger branches were left outside the front door in an effort to preserve the granny's sanity – but I think she nearly fainted the day she saw us struggling home with a six-foot-long branch balanced atop the buggy.

James began to make friends in the playground. Although they barely play together at this age, they do play side by side where they watch and observe each other closely. This is an important process which helps them learn social skills, preparing them for life at school and beyond. James was rather territorial at first, particularly about his bucket and spade. If anyone dared so much as touch it, I'm afraid they got walloped on the head with the spade. Most of the time I was able to see it coming and intercept before World War III broke out. Bearing in mind that distraction is the best prevention method at this age, I would point to the sky and shout, 'Aeroplane!' – or anything, really, to capture his attention. I would then remove him from the sandpit and sit him next to me for five minutes. One can't really reason with a two-year-old, so instant removal and distraction are the only tactics that work in this situation. One can, however, explain simply and calmly that hitting is forbidden; he soon learned from my stern tone of voice that it probably wasn't a good idea. After a few minutes we would return to the sandpit together and I would roll up my sleeves and involve both children in a new game. Soon enough the animosity would be forgotten and a new friendship formed.

The more fun James had with things, the happier and more vocal he became; his screams turned to speech and his vocabulary increased tremendously just by daily banter and chit-chat. I am a renowned chatterbox, which helps enormously with children of this age. James would copy what he heard and, on our gentle walks to the park, I would point out shops and ask James what was inside. What did they sell? As a car passed by, I'd ask what colour it was. How many people were inside? It added an element of fun and curiosity and kept James interested and alert.

The simple act of exposing James to a varied assortment of different activities and places, and adding an element of fun into the equation, turned him into a much more cooperative child. His granny and mum became more confident with him, and more understanding of his needs. Granny often came on outings with us and actually enjoyed rather than dreaded them. She learned to know his expectations and limits, and even began taking him along to visit her friends once again; this time, however, she knew to take along a few of his toys to amuse him, and would only stay for half an hour. I hear he behaved beautifully until he was offered a broken biscuit and pulled the cat's tail in frustration! The moral of the story? Never offer a two-year-old a broken biscuit …

SIBLING RIVALRY

There is never an easy way to introduce a new baby into a toddler's life. They will suddenly have to come to terms with the fact that they are no longer the centre of your universe. I have worked for many families when a new baby has been introduced, and it is definitely a time of transition for everyone concerned. The dynamics of the family change completely: attention has to be shared and more energy has to be found as you juggle between the new baby and the energetic toddler, all the while trying to make sure that everyone feels loved, cared for and special. I am always struck by how well families cope in this situation. Admittedly, those that I have observed have a certain amount of help in the form of yours truly, but ultimately a child wants their parents' attention, no matter how many lollipops I have in my pocket.

Children between the ages of one and two and a half do not fully understand the concept or implications of a new baby. At about the sixth month of pregnancy, you can tell them that Mummy has a baby in her tummy that belongs to all of you, and that your toddler is going to be a big brother or a big sister. Children of this age have no sense of time, and will probably then ask you most days if the baby is coming today. Older children have a little bit more of an understanding about babies arriving, and will possibly worry that they will disturb their peace. First responses range from 'Yuk!' to 'It had better be a boy' (if your toddler is male) or 'It had better be a girl' (if your toddler is female).

In one of the families I worked for, as soon as the new baby was born we made a timeline – a pictorial reference for the elder toddler. I gathered photographs of her from when she was newborn up until the present day, placed them along the timeline and wrote underneath what she was able to do at what age. She absolutely loved it. It gave her an insight into what to expect from the new baby when it was brought home, and we hung it on her wall for her to follow.

Because the toddler may not be used to their mother being away, it is essential that they should visit the hospital as soon as is possible after the baby is born. Try to make sure you are not feeding when they arrive, and pass the baby straight to your partner so that you can make a big fuss of your toddler on their arrival. It is a good idea to prepare a gift for the toddler to be given as soon as they see the baby – tell them that it's a gift from the baby. You will see that they will be quite curious at first, and might want a poke or two at the new baby. But that will be short-lived, and they will soon find something new to explore. Keep the visit short and sweet.

Visit the hospital as soon as possible

When bringing the baby home, the mother should let her partner or a friend carry the baby in so that she can greet her toddler with open arms. This may be the first time your toddler has ever seen you with another baby, so there might be tears and tantrums to deal with until they adapt. Give your toddler lots of cuddles and kisses to reassure them that they are special and loved. Try not to make a fuss of the baby in front of them and, when visitors arrive with a new present for the baby, let your toddler open it and play with it for a while. If they show an interest in the baby, let them be your little helper – encourage them to fetch and carry stuff and generally be a part of it all. However, don't expect this to happen. Most older siblings I have watched tend to ignore new babies as they are so busy with their own lives.

Keep your toddler's schedule the same as before the baby was born. This will offer some stability in a world which is changing for them. Make sure they have their trips to the park and playgrounds to play with friends. Struggle along with the new baby and

Keep the
usual
schedule

introduce it to your toddler's friends to encourage them to feel proud of it. There will undoubtedly be awkward moments when you need to feed the baby and your toddler wants you to play with them. Never say no, just try and make the baby part of the game. One little four-year-old girl I knew would pretend to be a cat every time I gave the baby her bottle. It endeared her to the baby and she resented the time I spent with it less and less. Another three-year-old boy I knew was extremely jealous until I appealed to his sense of humour by chasing him with the baby's nappy. He thought this was hilarious, and often asked to play the stinky nappy game. One day when he wanted to play Peter Pan, I dressed the baby up as Tinkerbell. He was enthralled, and so was she.

When the new baby becomes a bit more interesting and capable – probably around the age of six months – your toddler might start to become a little violent. You should never leave your toddler alone with the baby, as they do not know their own strength or capabilities. One doting father I worked with took his newborn baby and his two-year-old out to the park side by side in a double buggy. He stopped at a crossing to find the baby lying on the ground and the toddler with a contented little grin on her face. He could not believe his darling little girl could push the baby out like that. Believe it: they will. Once your baby starts sitting up and cooing, they will demand a lot more attention from you and from others. This will annoy your toddler and may provoke hitting or shoving to get the baby out of the limelight. Unless you can divert this before it happens, your only recourse is to make it perfectly clear to your toddler that such behaviour is totally unacceptable. They must go and sit on the stairs for a few minutes and learn that you will not tolerate hitting or violence. If they are younger than two, of course, they will not understand the implications of what they are doing, so you must just remove them from the room.

When the baby begins to crawl, trouble will really start. Chances are they will crawl into the middle of the elder toddler's game and knock down whatever it is they are playing with. You must respect the elder toddler's play area and not expect them to be sympathetic to or understanding of the baby. You will need to distract the baby, or pick them up and whisk them out of trouble. Give them their own toys to explore.

Some toddlers, especially as they get older, may want to be treated like a baby again. They might demand their own bottle, or ask to be carried like a baby. I once found a four-year-old girl forcing herself into a newborn's babygro and climbing into its pram – fortunately the baby wasn't in it at the time. I tend to play along with this – it is part of their way of trying to understand and deal with the new situation.

Younger siblings tend to worship elder siblings. As soon as the little one can sit up and watch, the elder toddler will become their idol. They will delight in attention from the elder sibling, so encourage this and tell the toddler that they are the baby's favourite person. They will revel in this, and entertain the baby with funny faces and noises. Soon enough they will grow to be friends, and play together just as much as they fight together.

My experience is that siblings fight fifty per cent of the time and play fifty per cent of the time. I believe that fighting is just another form of entertainment for them, and derives from some sort of animalistic desire to be chief of the clan. Most of the time I ignore it and let them sort it out between themselves. It's all part of learning to negotiate within a family structure; moreover, if you get involved it just becomes more of a drama. If I do need to get involved, I normally sort things out in such a way that I do not need to take sides. If they are fighting over a toy, I remove the toy so that they have to find something else to do. End of story.

If either of the children start to get violent, I separate them both so that they can calm down. When they are ready, I get them to apologise to each other. Mostly, arguments are caused by boredom, so I try to pre-empt them by suggesting we play something new and exciting. Earplugs help, too!

Organisation is essential In order to look after two children of different ages at the same time, you have to be organised. Now more than ever, structure and routine will help you cope with the enormity of it all. The elder child will – and should – receive the majority of your attention if you are juggling the care of a newborn baby as well. Your newborn will be happy just so long as they are fed, changed and cuddled enough; the elder child needs more verbal and intellectual stimulation.

It is best to introduce the newborn to all facets of the elder child's life as soon as you can. This will happen quite naturally as you carry them around with you and sit them on your lap as you play games with and chat to your elder child. When you have to give your newborn more attention – such as when you are feeding – let the elder child cuddle up as well and read a story or play a game together. If the elder child insists that you put the baby down while you are feeding, tell them you will do as soon as you have finished. Then, when you do, talk to the baby and say out loud that you have to put them down because you are busy playing with their elder brother or sister.

Gradually it will become easier as you synchronise the two schedules so that their nap times coincide and their feeding times match. You can bath them together, just so long as you gather all the items you will need beforehand so you never have to leave. Lie the baby on a towel, pop you toddler into the bath first and see to all their needs before putting the baby in. Remember to hold the baby at all times to protect them from the toddler's excited splashes, although often the baby will just be so enthralled by the antics of the toddler they won't mind having to put up with a little water in the face. Remove the baby first, dry and dress them and then see to the toddler. More often than not they entertain each other in these situations; this will help you become more relaxed and able to enjoy them both at the same time.

Double buggies are very handy items. I prefer the ones where the children sit in front of each other rather than side by side, as they are easier to manoeuvre through doorways and into lifts. Your upper body is in for quite a workout as the pair of them get bigger and heavier. There are wonderful devices called buggy boards that clip on to the back of a single buggy. They rather resemble skateboards, and your toddler can stand on them for a ride. These are particularly useful for the elder child who is willing to walk one way to the park but not on the way back home. They are also quite cool-looking, so they can help inspire a toddler who may be reluctant to give up their buggy.

During this busy time, enlist the help of your partner by asking them to pick up food on the way home from work and be prepared to make dinner. At the weekends, let them take the elder child off on special outings together – even if it is only to the garage or the supermarket. Suggest they have lunch or tea out together, so that you can enjoy one-on-one time together with your new baby. Relax for a few hours with the baby; don't get busy doing housework.

You should only put your new baby in the same room as your toddler if the elder one is still in a cot. That way, the new baby is safely protected from the curiosity of your toddler, who will want to have a bit of a poke around. Generally, toddlers become desensitised to the baby's crying, and learn to sleep through it. However, if your baby is waking your toddler constantly, it is important to remove the baby from the bedroom for a couple of weeks while you sort out their sleeping habits. You can place the baby's cot in a hallway or in the bathroom. Explain to your toddler that the baby needs to learn how to sleep through the night just like they do, and praise them for how well they do. You may need to explain that it is not their fault that the baby cries all night long – sometimes babies just do that, but when they stop they will come back to be their roommate.

Get your toddler to help

There are little things that you can do to help enhance the relationship between the toddler and the baby. In the early weeks, let them help you change nappies; examining poo seems to be toddlers' all-time favourite pastime! Let them choose what clothes the baby wears – even if it's not quite your cup of tea. Burping and winding will cause great giggles from your toddler. Let them gently pat the baby to see if they can rally a burp. Things will become easier as the baby becomes more responsive and smiles and coos lovingly at your toddler. Ask your toddler to sing songs and act out rhymes for your baby, who will very much appreciate it. All these little things will bring them closer together and relieve any jealously.

When the younger child is more mobile and constantly wants to be with their sibling and play with whatever they are playing with, you will need to be quick off the mark if you see them about to spoil the toddler's game. If you can't catch them in time, expect the elder child to retaliate with a thump or a smack. Try not to overreact if you see this happening; instead, pick up the younger child and comfort them, and explain to the elder child that hitting will not be accepted and that they need to learn to attract your attention if this happens again. Teach them how to offer something else of interest to the younger child to distract them from touching whatever it is they are playing with. Gradually the younger child will become tougher and learn the rules and, because they will be desperate to join in play with the elder child, they will learn what to touch and what not to touch. It's always comes as quite a shock when the younger child finally gives the elder one a good old wallop. Neither child can quite believe the shift in power, and you must comfort the elder child while telling the younger one that hitting is not acceptable. From then on you will notice that the power shift enables them to start playing together more comfortably.

You can help teach them how to play together by initiating games between all of you and making the elder child realise that the younger child can be fun and a part of things. Try playing a simple game of hide and seek: you hide with the younger child and let the elder child come and find you. Make sure the games you play are suitable for the younger child, and soon enough they will have worked out a way to play together. Don't put your peacekeeping hat away just yet, though!

MISS POPPY'S GUIDE TO HAVING FUN

Although you should be supervising your child all the time, that does not mean to say you have to spend every hour of the day entertaining them. Children of this age are naturally curious, and will often occupy themselves for a short while – perhaps ten or fifteen minutes – if they have a selection of toys to play with. They particularly enjoy sorting and emptying and then filling things up again, so a plastic bucket with a few empty cotton reels will keep them busy and entertained for some time. I often plop them down with something to play with while I go about doing my chores, moving them to whichever room I'm working in. It is a useful way of teaching them how to occupy themselves, and it does wonders for their concentration span. Being together constantly does not mean you have to entertain them constantly, and I think they enjoy the quiet times too. As long as they know you are there, they are happy to play away by themselves, and these can be very relaxing times for you both.

Most of the children I have come across dislike playpens as soon as they start becoming mobile, but this is not to say that they do not have their uses. They are great in situations where you have your hands full or are busy with an elder sibling and your baby is crawling towards something they should not be. Being able to restrict their movement and keep them in one spot, even for a short period of time, is invaluable. Along with a few amusing toys, your little one may be happy in a playpen for up to twenty minutes. Generally, however, they soon to learn to resent the playpen and will not tolerate it.

As your child grows, these quiet moments, I'm afraid, will become more and more precious. You will need to make sure that your toddler's days are filled with fun and stimulating activities, so here are a few ideas to help you do just that.

MISS POPPY'S GAMES FOR TODDLERS

Blow up a balloon and chase it around the room. Have some spares in case it pops!

Toddlers love ball games. Sit on the floor with a ball and roll it to each other. Go into the garden or park where you can kick it, throw it and chase it about

Trampoline sheets: place a ball or teddy or another cuddly toy on a sheet while holding all the sides with the help of however many toddlers you happen to have handy, and bounce it nice and high.

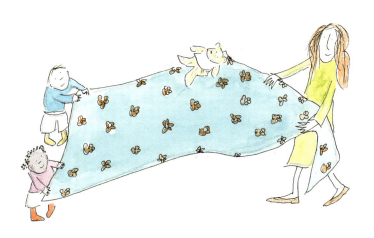

Toddlers also love to run under the bouncing trampoline

Hide a teddy or a favourite toy under a cushion or in a cupboard and encourage your child to find it. Remember to give them plenty of praise when they discover it

Scarf kites: tie a few scarves together – or you can use ribbons – and let your child run around, wafting their kite behind them

BUBBLES

All toddlers love it when you blow bubbles for them, or let them practise blowing their own. You can buy bottles of bubble solution, or you can make your own.

BUBBLE RECIPE

240ml (8floz) warm water
480ml (16floz) washing-up liquid
6 tablespoons glycerine (you can use sugar, but glycerine makes for longer-lasting bubbles)

Mix all the ingredients together and leave for three hours. Bubble wands can be made with pipe cleaners twisted into lollipop shapes.

TODDLER SANDWICHES

All you will need are two cushions or pillows and maybe a couple of tea towels. To make a toddler sandwich, pretend one of the cushions is a slice of bread, place your child on it, and then 'butter' vigorously by wiping your hand all over them. Add some lettuce or tomatoes in the form of tea towels, place the other slice of bread on top, then squeeze down for a guaranteed giggle.

ROLY-POLY TIME

Lay a towel out on top of the bed or on the floor, lie your child down on it with their arms by their sides like a soldier, wrap them up like a Swiss roll and then unravel them quickly so that they turn around.

HIDE AND SEEK

Let your child hide, even if it is behind the curtains every single time. Be animated and talk out loudly as you are seeking them. 'Where are you? Mmmm! I can smell you …' Act surprised when you find them.

MISS POPPY'S CREATIVE CRAFTS FOR TODDLERS

All crafts should be supervised by an adult at all times.

WATER PLAY

If you are playing inside at the sink, roll up their sleeves, place a towel on the ground and find a safe stool or chair for them to stand on. Fill the sink with warm bubbly water – the more washing-up liquid the better – and give them colanders, sponges, plastic funnels, cups, empty bottles, wooden spoons, ladles, empty yogurt pots and anything else that you think will add to the fun. They even enjoy washing their waterproof toys, dolls or action figures.

If you are outside and it is warm enough, fill up a paddling pool –

you can buy them cheaply enough. If not, fill a plastic bowl or bucket with warm water and give them an old paintbrush or sponge so that they can paint the outside of the house, outdoor furniture or even your car. They will love watering the garden with a watering can, or playing with a spray bottle or an old washing-up liquid bottle filled with water to squirt.

A SANDPIT

Make your own sandpit by filling a plastic paddling pool with sand. You could also use an old tyre, an old suitcase or even a wooden draw – just remember to cover it with a plastic sheet when it's not in use. Add buckets and spades, empty yogurt pots, sieves, colanders, scoops, spoons, shells and straws.

> *Hot sand pies to sell*
> *Hot sand pies to sell*
> *Pat them down tightly*
> *And turn them out well*

PLAY DOUGH

Play dough can be bought from most toy shops. Good tools for playing with it are a garlic press, a potato masher, wooden lollipop sticks, biscuit cutters, a rolling pin and sea shells.

BUSY BEE BOX (2 YEARS AND UP)

Keep a large cardboard box full of empty containers like biscuit tins with lids, cereal boxes, plastic Tupperware containers with lids, empty yogurt pots, empty paper towel rolls, tin foil or toilet rolls. Keep a separate tin with smaller objects like dried pasta, pebbles, old buttons, wooden beads, penny coins – but nothing too tiny. Hours of play will pass by as they fill up and empty cartons and tins, shake them to make a great noise, and measure and pour, all the time feeling the different shapes and sizes.

MUSICAL PLAY

Keep a selection of musical items in an area of the house or just in a box. Here are a few suggestions: a tambourine, a whistle, a recorder, a drum and drum sticks, a xylophone, maracas, a mini keyboard, a bell, some cymbals. Create your own noise-makers with empty baby formula or coffee tins with plastic lids. Wash them out so they are nice and fresh, sprinkle a few dried beans or peas inside, pop the lid back on and stick it firmly down with masking or duct tape.

ACTIVITY GROUPS

From the age of one year, you will find that there are a large number of activity groups for you and your child to attend. Music groups are a lot of fun for both of you. Mostly your child will sit on your lap, clap their hands and enjoy the musical stimulation. As they get slightly older, your child will benefit greatly from baby-gym classes. They offer an inside space with soft climbing structures set up at the right height for the children attending. Often a class will combine the music and the gym aspects, offering half an hour to play and exert their physical energy and half an hour to listen to music and dance. These classes are designed to help your child develop their coordination and confidence, and give them a heightened awareness of the world around them. They have always been very popular with the young toddlers I have cared for, and are an early introduction to a structured environment as well as a great place to meet friends.

CHAPTER THREE:
2½ – 5 years

'Oh, there's such a lot of things to do and such a lot to be.'
– Now We Are Six, A. A. MILNE

Your precious toddler is growing into a fully fledged little person who chatters away in full sentences and is able to express their feelings and emotions. Curiosity abounds. Why? What? Where? When? Soon they will be able to dress themselves, count their toes, eat with a knife and fork. They will learn how to be considerate to others and let them play with their toys. They will be able to peddle their tricycle faster and faster and chase ducks in the park. They will invent glorious stories of their escapades and you will have to clap and applaud. They will without doubt be wanting to join in with whatever it is you are doing – help is here! – and this is a great time to teach them a sense of responsibility by allowing them to help with daily chores.

In this chapter we will look at how your example will be the key to your child learning how to learn, and learning how to behave. We will then see how you can deal with the 'fussy-eater' stage that so many children of this age go through, and also how to cope with their ever-changing sleep patterns and the problems associated with bedwetting. As your child gets older, you may start thinking about nurseries or other types of childcare, so I have included a section about the various options available and how to choose the one that is right for you. To finish up, I have given you some more ideas about how to fill your growing child's days with creative, stimulating and enjoyable play.

LEARNING BY EXAMPLE

'Example isn't another way to teach, it is the only way to teach.'
— ALBERT EINSTEIN

I am a great believer that children will never learn to do anything for themselves unless we actively encourage them to do so. Toddlers absolutely love to get involved in whatever it is you are doing, whether it be dusting, sweeping or washing the dishes. You will find that they are always willing to help if you ask, and they must be rewarded with plenty of praise. It will boost their self-confidence no end. What might appear to us to be drudgery can be immense fun to a little one. Mopping the kitchen floor, for example, is an absolute favourite, and it works wonders for their coordination. I have spent many a rainy day with a three-year-old, a bucket of soapy water and a mop. They love swishing and sliding it across kitchen floors, stamping out any bubbles with their bare feet. But it is more than a game: by encouraging their involvement we are displaying acceptance and approval. They, in turn, grow in confidence and ability, and learn how to work together as a team.

Involve your toddler in a chore

Your child will gain an enormous sense of accomplishment if you allow them to perform simple everyday tasks such as helping to lay the table, sorting washing out into piles and putting it into the machine, dusting, polishing, vacuuming, tidying away their toys, making their bed, feeding the family pet, emptying the rubbish bins, drawing the curtains or helping to put the shopping away. Just because these are daily duties we do almost automatically, you must never expect perfection. Praise any attempt to help, however small and however long it may take – and it could take a while. It is important, though, never to rush them. Toddlers like to do things in their own time, even if it is light years away from yours.

I like to make a chart of daily chores for my toddlers so they can tick of all their daily tasks or choose which one they would like to do on any particular day. You can turn it into a game, especially if they are feeling a bit grumpy. Cover their eyes with a scarf, spin them around a couple of times and then let them point their finger at the list. Take the blindfold off and see where their finger has landed: that's their chore for today. To make your list, write down a selection of daily tasks that they are able to accomplish by themselves.

MISS POPPY'S CHORE LIST

Feed the family pet

Empty the waste-paper bin

Mop the floor

Dust and polish

Tidy up their toys with your help

Set their place setting at the table

Sort out the washing into piles

Pair the socks and put them away

Help load or unload the dishwasher and learn where things belong

Draw the curtains or blinds

Straighten their bed and line up all the soft toys and teddies

Bring their dirty washing to the washing machine

By involving your toddler and asking for their help, you are showing them how much you value them, how they are a part of a family and that you all have to pull together to make things work. I have found that children who learn to do things for others at an early age continue to do so as they are growing up. They learn to care about and value people, which increases their understanding of and empathy for others. It is an important part of life, but it is easy to forget that it has to be nurtured and taught by us and our example. Let your child see you make a point of helping people who are struggling with buggies and babies on the bus. Let them see you give up your seat to an elderly person or pregnant lady on public transport. Explain why you are doing it, and point out how much more difficult it is for them to get around. Encourage your child to make a get-well card for a friend, or to draw a picture to cheer them up. They could even help you bake a cake or some biscuits to deliver to them. Your toddler will feel delighted and proud of their good deed. Praise them for all their help and kindness and allow them to see how good it made the recipient feel.

LETTERS AND NUMBERS

By the age of three, your child may start showing an interest in learning their ABC and how to count. There are many fun ways to encourage and enhance this without ever forcing the issue.

A great way of teaching the alphabet is to cut out A–Z in large letters, preferably in a textured material such as corrugated cardboard. I tend to place the large cut-out letters alphabetically in a row all around the room or up on a pinboard so that they are visible. Alternatively, you can buy wonderful charts and posters of illustrated alphabets which look great on a child's wall. Flash cards also work well, as does an alphabet book. Let your child copy the shapes on a plain pad of paper in order to become familiar with each letter, and teach them how to sing the traditional ABC song to the tune of 'Twinkle Twinkle Little Star'.

With your set of letters there are lots of fun games you can play together. Let your child choose a letter at random, for example, and then find something beginning with that letter. Or you can move through the letters alphabetically, finding things that begin with each letter. Try playing alphabet snap with two sets of A–Z flash cards. Shuffle each set and have one set each. Place cards alternately face-up until there is a repeated letter. The first person to shout 'Snap!' wins all the cards in the pile, and the game continues until one person runs out of cards. Many children I have cared for have enjoyed a magnetic alphabet stuck on the fridge – while I'm busy cooking I jumble them up and ask them to find a certain letter. Floating letters and numbers are also great for the bath.

To begin teaching numbers, try to present your child with opportunities to sort objects into groups. They could separate socks into groups of colour and size, or separate items of fruit in a fruit bowl. Ask them to count how many items are in each group. Which group has the most? Which group has the least? Coins are also fun to sort out into piles and groups. If you collect change in a jar, empty it all out on to the table and let your child sort out the different colours, shapes and sizes into piles. A child's room is full of opportunities to play sorting and counting: cars and trucks, for example, can be grouped by shape, size and colour. And farm sets are ideal: sort out the animals and livestock – pigs, cows, sheep, ducks – and then count them up to see which animal you have the most of. A favourite game is playing shop. Set up a shop front using a table and let your child raid the kitchen cupboards to choose what they would like to sell in their shop. If you have a toy cash till, so much the better; if not, some coins neatly arranged in piles will do just as well. You pretend to be the customer, and let your child count out your purchases and your change.

TIDY TODDLERS

'What are you able to build with your blocks?
Castles and palaces, temples and docks.
Rain may keep raining, and others go roam,
But I can be happy and building at home.'
– *Block City*, ROBERT LOUIS STEVENSON

In teaching children responsibility for their own toys and belongings, one has to be slightly more imaginative when it comes to encouraging their help. But I have learned that if you sprinkle an element of fun into the mix, you will be rewarded with eager participation.

I am convinced that an organised room leads to an organised child, and being organised will be such a useful skill throughout their life. Begin by establishing a time at the end of the day – either just before or just after bath time when most of the day's serious playing is over – and call it 'clean-up time'. Invent a signature song or put on a favourite CD and sing along, using the same one night after night. If your child is deeply engrossed in play, don't fully interrupt their game and bring it to an abrupt halt, as this will only be cause for tears of frustration. Instead, try to include whatever it is they are playing into the clean-up game. Always try to smooth transitions with playful thoughts and ideas so as to encourage your toddler rather than infuriate them. So, if they are busy playing pretend restaurants, suggest that it's time to get the bill and clear the tables. If they are playing with an action figure, suggest that it might be time for his bath.

Make 'clean-up time' fun

A word of advice: don't be over-enthusiastic in your cleaning up. If your child has created an elaborate building, for example, and has been working on it for some time, it may be a masterpiece work in progress and should be regarded as such. I once had to tiptoe around a charge's room as he had turned the whole floor into an elaborate road system. He noticed every single millimetre I moved a car. His elaborate designs and inventive engineering took days to create and therefore deserved great respect from all who wandered near them.

MISS POPPY'S CLEAN-UP SONGS

TIME TO PUT MY TOYS AWAY

This should be sung to the tune of 'London Bridge is Falling Down'.

It's time to put my toys away
Toys away
Toys away
It's time to put my toys away
For the day is done

ARE YOU HELPING?

This should be sung to the tune of 'Frère Jacques'.

Are you helping
Are you helping
Pick up toys
Pick up toys?
Let us all be helpers
Let us all be helpers
Girls and boys
Girls and boys

There are many imaginative and inventive ways to organise your child's toys neatly, and I always enlist my charges' help in doing this – even if they are more interested in playing with toys newly rediscovered under the bed or at the back of a cupboard. One way is to organise your shelves, drawers or boxes into various colours – you could paint them different colours or decorate them with coloured stickers. I like to make a poster that helps teach toddlers their colours and shapes. Paint a big blue circle, for example, and next to it draw pictures of all the things that go on the blue shelf or in the blue box – let's say puzzles and board games. Your toddler can help you by placing blue stickers on all the items that go on the blue shelf. Next comes yellow. On the poster I draw a big yellow square and pictures of all the items that go on the yellow shelf or box – building bricks and blocks, for example. All the building bricks and blocks get yellow stickers. The green shelf or box can be for toy cars, trucks and trains. Add a green triangle to your poster and don't forget to get your toddler to help stick green stickers on all the relevant toys. The red shelf can be for stuffed animals, dolls and action figures. Repeat the same procedure as before, and don't forget to add a red rectangle to your poster.

The list of things you can organise is almost endless, and it makes clean-up time so much easier – and much more fun – if you play the following clean-up game, which also helps teach your toddler their colours.

MISS POPPY'S CLEAN-UP COLOUR GAME

During clean-up time, you or your toddler must request a colour – let's say red. You and your toddler have to find all the toys that belong on the red shelf or in the red box and put them back where they belong. For an added bit of healthy competition, see who can get the most red items. You could add a bit of zest for the older toddler by using a stopwatch to time how long it takes them to find all the red toys that need to be put away. Before you know it you have a tidy room and happy child. If you want to make it really challenging, intermittently change which colour they should be looking for. This is always cause for giggles and shrieks of delight, and it is a fun way to learn colours.

The way you design your toddler's room will have a great impact on how successfully they can keep their things tidy. In my time I have seen many children's rooms, ranging from the elaborate fairy-tale-princess-style, complete with four-poster bed and life-size

Barbie doll (very scary), to a simple child's hammock swinging between trees built around a wooden hut in Cambodia. I once worked for a marvellous family of four who all lived in one room and each had their own individual style emphasised in their corner.

When designing a toddler's room, get down on your knees and see things from their perspective. This is their room, and so has to be comfortable for someone of their size. A low bed with a duvet covered in a novelty cover and pillow case immediately adds life to the room. It is also much easier for your toddler to learn how to make their bed with a duvet rather than with sheets and blankets. Sliding drawers under the bed make excellent storage for toys or clothes, and are easily reachable for your toddler. A low child-size table and chair positioned near low bookshelves provides a work and play area, and the shelves can store books which they can easily reach and put back. How about a shelf to display their latest collection of rocks, stones or empty cartons – whatever it is they have discovered that captures their interest this week? Or a shelf to store all their stuffed animals? A shelf for musical instruments?

A large pinboard covering a wall works well for displaying paintings they have done, or photographs of family members and friends. Tell them stories about people in your family – it will be a way of sharing history and they will especially like stories about you when you were little and what you got up to. Make sure your toddler can reach it and is encouraged to display all their creative masterpieces so that they can be seen – and praised – by everyone. One little chap I knew made the most elaborate drawings for his overworked father, who kindly took them and placed them in his drawer for safe-keeping. When the little boy stopped drawing, I had a quiet word with his father, who framed the drawings and proudly displayed them all over his study. Few words were said, but in this case actions spoke louder: the little chap started drawing again.

Place hooks at your toddler's height behind doors so that they can hang up their coats, clothes and pyjamas. Create a simple sense of order so that they can quickly and easily find what it is that they are looking for without the place looking like a bombsite. In time they will learn their own sense of order by putting things back where they belong. And remember to respect the fact that it is their room, a place where their individuality should shine and freedom of expression be encouraged.

After all, you can always shut the door.

GETTING DRESSED

At this age, you should start to encourage your toddler to dress themselves in order to nurture their independence. Start by letting them get undressed by themselves at bath time – taking clothes off is much easier for a toddler than putting them on. A good way to start your toddler learning to dress themselves is by teaching them the flip-coat technique. Lay their coat out on the floor, upside down and with the inside facing them, place their arms inside the sleeves and let them lift up the coat and throw it over their head while pushing their arms into the armholes. Hey presto – they have put their own coat on. They may need help

Start with undressing rather than dressing

with the buttons or zip, but they will have taken their first step in dressing themselves.

Children should have a say in what they wear, and you can expect a very individual creative streak to become apparent by the age of three. This need not become a battleground if you are a bit savvy. One charge of mine insisted on wearing full party regalia every single day for about six weeks. It was the party dress or nothing, and she would trot off to nursery every morning dressed to kill. I hand-washed that dress more times than I care to remember, and learned a very valuable lesson: anything inappropriate should be put out of sight and only brought out for special occasions. A selection of decent everyday clothes should be left hanging and folded neatly in drawers or on shelves so that your child may exert their independence and choose what to wear.

If you have the space, hang all their clothes on a low-level rod so that they can see things clearly. They will undoubtedly pull out every single T-shirt and rummage through every item of clothing before they find what they are looking for, so it is a good idea to teach them how to roll their clothes up rather than expect them to be able to fold things up – this is an impossible task even for many adults I have met. Rolling T-shirts and other clothes still keeps them neat and wearable, and they will stack nicely into drawers.

Let them choose tomorrow's outfit before going to bed. I have invented a game to help them do this.

MISS POPPY'S ALPHABET CLOTHES GAME

Not only will this game encourage them to dress themselves, it will help them start to learn the alphabet. On each draw or shelf, draw a picture of the items that belong there. For example, if it's an underwear, vest and sock draw, draw a picture of a vest with the letter V next to it, some socks with a letter S and some underwear with a letter U. Don't worry about the quality of your drawings, just so long as they are clear and recognisable – although Polaroids could be used if you prefer. Do the same for wardrobes and other drawers and shelves. Shoes can even have a lower shelf or the bottom of the wardrobe.

The game begins by you asking your toddler to lay out the outfit they want to wear. You could do this when they are getting dressed in the morning, or they could lay out their clothes for the next day last thing at night (this has the added advantage of preventing any last-minute panics first thing in the morning, which invariably lead to you digging through the dirty washing and fishing out their favourite T-shirt for the fifth day in a row). Request a U for underwear, an S for shirt, a T for trousers and continue the game until the outfit is all laid out on the floor or at the bottom of their bed ready to leap into.

If you can arrange things so that when they wake up in the morning they have no major choices or decisions, they will be more likely to get on with dressing themselves as soon as they wake up. Of course, you must hang around and offer help, but wait to be asked and praise any attempt they may have made, even if their shirt is on upside down and backwards. Tell them what an excellent job they have done and quietly suggest that it may be more comfortable if you just adjust it a little bit. Remember: practice makes perfect.

Arrange clothes the night before

LEARNING TO BE GOOD

'To be great is to be misunderstood.' – RALPH WALDO EMERSON

Toddlers need their day to be structured and varied if they are to remain occupied, interested and cooperative. At times, though, they will challenge you in each and every way they can, and you will find yourself exasperated, exhausted and defeated by this little tyrant only as tall as your knees. Don't worry. This stage is normal, and although it is probably one of the most challenging, it will pass – as long as you stand firm.

Keep consistent rules

Limits and boundaries have to be clearly set and adhered to in order for your toddler to feel safe and secure. Consistency is the name of the game here: you must not confuse your toddler by constantly changing the rules. Children flourish with familiarity, and too many changes will cause massive insecurities which will manifest themselves in the form of physically challenging tantrums and general all-round bad behaviour. If you don't deal with it firmly now, it may well lead to learning problems and social isolation further down the road, an inability to make friends and low self-esteem. If your toddler is using tantrums as a means of getting their own way, you need to put a stop to it right now.

As your toddler grows bigger and their verbal skills increase, tantrums can become less and less easy to cope with. There is no reason why you shouldn't still use the technique of distraction that we discussed in the previous chapter (see page 128), but between the ages of three and four you may find that they are less likely to respond to this technique. Once they know the power of their own voice, they will use it if they don't get their own way. It can be scary for you – and the whole neighbourhood! – when they do this. When they reach this stage, I have found that prevention is better than cure.

Think about when tantrums occur

Remember that tantrums are caused by insecurities, unmet needs and frustration. Observe your toddler closely and examine when and where the tantrums occur. Is it always last thing at night before they are absolutely exhausted? If so, they need to go to bed earlier, or their nap needs to be longer during the day. Is it at the sweet counter in a shop when you refuse to buy them sweets? If so, try to avoid sweet counters or be prepared to offer them a small snack – a biscuit or a couple of Smarties – just before you enter the shop to keep them occupied. If tantrums are occurring before meal times, you need to bring meal times forward by half an hour, or make sure you offer a selection of healthy snacks throughout the day to keep their energy levels up.

If tantrums are happening at the supermarket, allow your toddler to choose something when you first begin shopping – a special packet of cereal, perhaps. Most supermarkets now prepare fresh fruit, and I have found that a few peeled grapes in a small lunch pack, complete with a plastic fork, occupies and amuses them for a while. And if you find that they create a fuss at the checkout – probably because they have seen the sweets on display – just ignore it as best you can. Look around you – there are probably four more tantrums taking place. Try (and this may not be easy if you are laden down with shopping) to take your toddler outside and bend down to their level. Look directly into their eyes and explain calmly and clearly, but in a firm manner, that this behaviour is not acceptable. Mostly, if they come out of the shop empty-handed after a series of tantrums, they eventually give up.

Toddlers need a certain amount of physical play to burn off all that excess energy. Tantrums often occur because there is no outlet for them to do this. If the weather is fine, go outside and play chasing and catching each other in the garden or local park or playground. If it's pouring down with rain, let them jump up and down on the bed or chase them around the house.

On the other hand, you might find tantrums occurring in the middle of a busy day between, say, swimming lessons and playgroup. It might be that your toddler is absolutely exhausted and you are expecting too much from them too soon. It is their way of saying they need some quiet time simply to play happily alone in the comfort of their own home. It is tempting to keep toddlers' days packed full of exciting activities as they seem to have an endless amount of energy, but be careful: they are still little and are absorbing and processing enormous amounts of information every day. They need precious time at home to digest that information and relax. Over time you will learn to recognise your toddler's limits by listening to and understanding their needs.

MISS POPPY'S PRE-TANTRUM TAMERS
Have a gentle pillow fight
Go outside and kick a ball around
Lie on the ground and play gentle wrestling
Jump on the bed
Play chase and catch inside or out
Put on a bouncy cd and dance and jump to the music
Get on all fours and chase them around the house

BRAVE, ENERGETIC NANNY NEEDED FOR FOUR CHILDREN – NEWBORN BABY GIRL, TWO-YEAR-OLD BOY, FOUR-YEAR-OLD BOY AND SIX-YEAR-OLD GIRL – FOR SUMMER HOLIDAY IN REMOTE SCOTTISH HIDEAWAY. MUST BE SPORTY, OUTGOING AND SELF-RELIANT.

I first met the Campbell clan in London during the interview. In retrospect I think they must have bribed their children into good behaviour as they seemed, at first sight, relatively normal. Their parents were very entertaining and jovial, and were most open and honest about the number of nannies they had been through. I think it was about ninety-eight at that point. But because of their humour, and because I had been presented with a challenge, I accepted the position and set off for a busy, fun-packed summer in the remote Western Islands of Scotland.

It was within an hour of getting to know each other that I experienced the first major tantrum. Tom, the four-year-old boy, had taken to biting his two-year-old brother Sam quite viciously. Both of them were screaming at the top of their voices and they were trying to pull each other's hair out. I managed to pull them apart and remove Tom from the room. His body went limp and he kicked and screamed, biting me in the process. Talk about a baptism of fire – I wanted to grab my bag, which was still unpacked, and head for the hills. I stayed with Tom while he kicked and screamed for a good forty-five minutes and tried desperately to get back into the room where his brother was. He reminded me of an attacking crocodile as he flipped his body back and forth. There was nothing to do but let him act it all out. When he began whimpering, I knew it was nearly over. I brought him to my lap and just soothed and cuddled him without saying a word about what had just happened. When he seemed calm, I took him for a little walk around the garden to freshen him up and for a change of scene.

That, I'm afraid, was just the beginning. Over the next three days the children clocked up eight to twelve tantrums a day between them. It was very ugly, demanding, violent and exhausting. Luckily their parents were present and willing to step in and help at any time, but they were still quite preoccupied with their newborn baby girl, Ella, who was only four weeks old. It was like walking on eggshells – you never quite knew why, when or where they were going to create. The simplest of things would start them off, such as apple juice for breakfast instead of orange juice. Sam once threw a massive tantrum because it was raining when he didn't want it to. Tom would scream a stream of sophisticated abuse if you did not purchase what he wanted when visiting the nearby village shops. I would often find a 'closed' sign greeting us if they saw us coming down the lane – I fear their reputation preceded them. Annie, the six-year-old girl, went crazy whenever I tried to switch off the television.

I really felt at my wits' end with these children, and several times I nearly gave up. One time I got as far as packing my bag; their mother was unpacking it at the same time, begging me to stay.

For the next two weeks I watched all the children closely and tried to understand where their bad behaviour stemmed from. I knew their parents' focus had shifted slightly with the arrival of Ella, and so it was natural that they should all regress slightly due to the jealously a new baby in the house creates. The parents had chosen to deal with it by suspending all limitations on the children's behaviour – possibly to relieve their guilt and to try and make the children feel that they were still cherished and loved. But setting no limits or boundaries had the opposite effect. They were bought new toys every time they went somewhere – bags of sweets at the petrol station, a garden gnome at the garden centre – and they didn't care what it was or even have any interest in most things they were given. They were often left on the back seat of the car or out in the garden to rust in the rain. Outings became unbearable as they insisted on visiting the gift shop first and wanted to buy every single item in the shop. You would be amazed at what there is to buy in the remote Scottish islands, and refusals lead to megalithic tantrums which frightened the life out of me.

Broken toys were immediately replaced with new toys, so the children never learned to respect or value anything. Most worryingly, they discovered that violent tantrums were a means of moving parental attention away from the new baby. They did not care that it was negative attention – it was attention from their parents all the same. And the high turnover of nannies just increased their insecurities: they did not feel loved or good about themselves. It was a vicious cycle for the nannies, the parents and the children.

I spoke in great depth with the parents, who were desperate at this point, and we discussed ways of handling tantrums and how to prevent them happening in the first place. I requested that they were to be given no more toys for the whole summer holidays. Bad behaviour was to be punished by restricting things they liked doing, such as watching television and playing video games. In any case these were to be restricted to an hour a day as I was convinced they were causing pent-up physical energy and frustration. We agreed that the children needed a lot more outdoor play and activity to release some of that physical energy which was manifesting itself in the form of tantrums. And we all had to be consistent and follow through with our decisions – no verbal threats, just immediate action. I also insisted that it was important that both parents spent individual time with each child without Ella's presence so that they felt valued, loved and cherished. In turn this would help the other children accept baby Ella as part of their family, and make them realise that not much had changed – their parents were still there to take care of them.

We chose to deal with tantrums with 'time out' – time out of the room for both child and adult to calm down. When the child was ready to deal with it, they were allowed to come and sit with you and try to explain using words what had happened. Physically nasty tantrums were handled by just walking away from the disruptive child, trying your best to ignore them and getting on with something, even if they followed you from room to room clinging on to your legs. You just took lots of deep breaths and tried to remain calm and insisted on no communication until the tantrum was well and truly over. Afterwards you always cuddled and made up.

I introduced behaviour charts with smiley faces – one chart for each child so that they had something to aim for. I listed simple tasks and areas of behaviour they all needed to work on:

No getting up in the morning before it's light

Get dressed before breakfast

No fighting during meals times

Help set the table

No rude names or language

Speak nicely to each other

Be polite to adults

Park all outside toys, bikes and scooters in the shed at the
    end of the day

Remember your manners and always say 'please' and 'thank you'

At the end of each day we filled in the chart together and tried to focus on the positive improvements that day rather than the negative ones. If one child was not doing partiularly well in one area, we didn't say much and moved on to the area they were improving in and placed a smiley face there. At the end of the week we counted up how many smiley faces each child had gained and set them a goal for the following week.

I encouraged the children to sort out their disagreements with words not fists by getting them to sit on the 'disagreement chairs' – I set up two chairs opposite each other along with pens and paper in what we called the 'disagreement area' and, when they felt like they were about to lose it with each other, encouraged them to sit down and use words, pictures or drawings to describe how they felt. This often led to giggles instead of tears as they drew crazy pictures of each other.

Over the summer I felt their self-esteem improved a great deal. This led to fewer outbursts and much more cooperative behaviour in general. The limits and boundaries were very clear, precise and consistent. They knew exactly what was expected of them and this offered them a great deal more safety and security. This in turn led to a more bearable, even enjoyable Scottish summer for us all – and even the local shops greeted us with an 'open' sign once more!

Dealing with tantrums can be very stressful for both you and your toddler. You need to be firm and consistent every time a tantrum occurs by repeating the same procedure. If you choose to ignore them, continue to do so. Walk out of the room when they begin *Be firm and* and try to busy yourself with a task. Continue to ignore them *consistent* when they follow you around, making it clear there will be no communication until the screaming and crying stops. When they are ready to stop, you can comfort them and move on. If they wish to talk about it, let them express their feelings on the matter, then calmly explain that it would be better if they could use words next time. Move on as quickly as you can: although it may be difficult, try never to dwell on a tantrum.

If you find yourself unable to ignore them and they manage to press every one of your buttons, the best thing to do is to call 'time out', as I did with the Campbell clan. Choose a room or safe place to send your toddler while you both calm down. I tend not to send them to their room, as there are too many fun things to play with! Instead I put them at the bottom of the stairs or out in the corridor – that way no door has to be shut, they feel less isolated and you can keep a close eye on them. When the tantrum begins, immediately state that time out has begun and take action. Carry them, if needs be, to another room or space, and tell them they need time to calm down before you will discuss anything with them. Then immediately leave the area. Don't get drawn into a conversation during the tantrum as this will only escalate matters. If they follow you, keep on returning them again and again, but offer no verbal communication.

As for you, just take lots of deep breaths, drink a glass of water and *Stay calm!* stick your head out of the door for a gulp of fresh air. Do what you need to do to stay calm as this can be a very emotionally draining experience indeed.

When you feel ready, and your toddler has calmed down, you can comfort them and discuss what the problem was. If the tantrum starts up all over again, repeat the same procedure. Remember: no communication until the screaming and crying have stopped.

If you are not at home when a tantrum starts, you need to remove your child as quickly as possible from the place where they are playing up. If you are in a department shop or at a friend's house, take them to the bathroom and close the door. Get down to their level and look directly into their eyes so they know you mean business. Say to them in a firm, clear voice that this is to stop. If they do not stop, you may just have to sit there and suffer until the tantrum passes.

When the crying finishes, take your toddler straight home and make a point of explaining to them that if tantrums occur while you are out shopping or visiting, that's the end of the trip. The message will soon hit home if you are consistent. The next time you are out and find yourself on the verge of a tantrum, remind them that you will have to go home if the tantrum begins – this is normally enough to nip it in the bud if they know you mean what you say.

MINDING YOUR PS AND QS

If tantrums are not stopped early, they can lead to general bad behaviour and rudeness. If you find your toddler being downright rude to you or to others, you need to take immediate action – it is completely unacceptable behaviour and will not make your toddler popular, especially with children of their own age.

Rudeness is not to be accepted at any level. If your toddler is rude to you or to others, step in immediately. Get down to their level, look directly into their eyes and in a firm voice explain that you are very upset with them and that this is not how you speak to people. I also make them go and sit on the stairs in sort of a time-out procedure. Take away whatever it is they are playing with at that moment, or stop any fun activity they are doing, and insist they sit there to think about their behaviour. Explain to them that when they are ready to apologise they may move from the stairs. If this initiates a tantrum then immediately kick into fully fledged time out. After they have calmed down, suggest they make a nice picture or drawing to give to the person they were rude to. This normally smoothes things over nicely. If they are allowed to get away with rude behaviour the first time, they will continue to repeat it until they are stopped. And if you don't stop them, someone else will – much to your toddler's embarrassment and shame. It is much better that you take the responsibility and deal with it rather than leaving it up to someone else.

Don't ever let them get away with rudeness

If their behaviour does not improve, you may withhold things they like: no television, no weekly trips to the ice-cream shop, no playing with their favourite building blocks. Be firm and set a clear boundary. Nobody likes a rude child.

You can create a behavioural smiley-face chart as I did with the Campbells to help encourage them to behave better. List all the areas of behaviour they need to work on, and at the end of each day you can fill it in together, drawing a smiley face at all the entries where they improved and tried hard. Don't focus on the negative aspects – just pass them by quickly and concentrate on the positive aspects of their improving behaviour. Make a big fuss of them when they receive a smiley face so they feel good about themselves.

Children learn by example: they copy what they see. Most of the extreme cases of rude and physically violent children I have experienced have derived from what they have observed around them. Often they will have witnessed violent acts by watching television and videos way beyond their emotional capacity to comprehend and capability to digest. When toddlers don't understand something, they act it out again and again to try and help them to understand. One four-year-old boy I came across was allowed to watch adult horror movies which led to his violent outbursts at preschool and his ultimate suspension. Another little girl was allowed to watch scary dinosaur movies from the age of three; she dealt with her fears by acting out aggressive dinosaur-like behaviour on all her siblings. This is why it is very important you supervise and edit everything your toddler sees on television. Cable TV is now ubiquitous, and most televisions have an attractive remote control with enticing coloured buttons to press. Your toddler will love it, but you must keep it out of reach at all times. I once walked in to find a two-year-old watching pornography, much to his parents' horror. They were in the kitchen at the time and were most embarrassed – I assume it was a subscription channel!

Be careful not to use television as a babysitter. I personally do not agree with television blaring in the background the whole day, especially when there are children around. Television, if used wisely, can be an enjoyable learning experience for your toddler – there are some wonderful music, song and rhyme videos for children that entertain and teach at the same time. But I do feel that at this age half an hour a day is an adequate amount of time to be spending in front of the TV. It makes for a good wind-down time: if you need your toddler to take a rest and just sit still for half an hour, pop on a musical video and watch and wind down together.

MANNERS

Simple, polite greetings to others can be taught to your toddler, and will stand them in great stead for the rest of their life. I always make a point of asking children of this age to say 'hello' to people. I take their hand, say my hello and then encourage the child to say theirs. Often it's just a wave or a sweet smile. If the child is meeting a new person, I introduce that person and then encourage the child to tell them their name. You should never force a child to speak, but if you set good examples they will gain confidence and copy your friendliness. I often meet new people in the playground, as do my charges. If we are playing in the sandpit with a new toddler friend, I make a point of asking their name and introducing my charge to them and then myself. Repeat the procedure when you say good-bye. If you are at somebody's house, explain to your toddler while you are getting ready to leave that it is time to say thank you. Don't force them or make a fuss – just set an example. If they adamantly refuse to say thank you or goodbye, explain that they will not be able to return to their friend's house in the future and play with all their lovely toys. This usually does the trick. Once they understand it, this behaviour should start to come naturally.

By the age of three and a half years, your toddler should be sharing and taking turns without making a fuss. You may have to supervise and explain whose turn it is now, but they will be happy to abide by the rules, and be the first to point out who is not. If the other

toddler seems reluctant, suggest that they have five minutes playtime each with a particular toy. It's usually long enough for them to have found something else of interest to play with.

If you find that sharing is still causing tears, tantrums and frustrations, it may be that your child has not been exposed to other children enough and therefore has not learned to share. Begin by heading out to the local playground and exposing your child to simple forms of sharing like having to wait for their turn on the slide, queue for the swing and establish which bucket is whose in the sandpit. They will soon learn the rules as they will *Sharing needs* be desperate to fit in and be part of the team. Next, invite friends *to be learnt* over to the house to play. Sharing their own personal toys may be hard at first. If they snatch everything out of the visitor's hand, try not to react too negatively. Suggest a game that you can all play together and ask if you can use their things because you need it for the game. When they agree, thank them and praise them for their generosity. Spend a lot of time making the guest feel as important as you can to compensate for your child's unwillingness to share.

Another tool I have used to enhance and practise sharing is an egg timer or a stopwatch. Each child gets a certain amount of time on each toy and we use the egg timer or stopwatch to time them. What usually happens is that it becomes more fun to operate the timer than play with the toy in question – but it seems to work wonders!

DEALING WITH BULLIES

When your child is exposed to another child's aggression or anger, your natural response is to be protective towards your child and remove them from the culprit as quickly as you can. Hopefully the other child's parent or carer will take responsibility and prompt the culprit to apologise. If they don't, feel free to approach them and explain, in a non-threatening way, what happened. Although I feel it is not my place to correct another person's child, I have at times stepped in and tried to explain to the aggressor that other children will not play with them if they hit them. Sometimes, by explaining the consequences of their actions very simply, their behaviour changes. Often they want to be friends with your little one, but are insecure and don't know how to go about it. If your child wishes to continue playing with them, allow it – but stay very close and supervise and intervene when need be before their behaviour turns physical. This is a good way of teaching your child how to deal with and solve problems.

I have encountered situations when my charge has been at the receiving end of bullying behaviour while at preschool. I only became aware of the problem when I noticed that the amount of laundry being sent home was increasing – his toilet skills were regressing and I sensed there was something going on at school. I spoke to the teachers, other parents and my charge and gradually pieced together what was happening. The aggressor was suffering behavioural problems because of his family circumstances and, as my charge was bubbly and bright, he wanted to be friends. Because of his large size and aggressive tendencies, however, my charge was frightened of him. A vicious circle had been created.

I spoke to the charge's parents, who met with the headmistress and discussed the escalating situation. Unfortunately, not enough was done to protect my charge and he ended up with stitches in his forehead because the aggressor threw something at him across the classroom. He was dismissed immediately, of course, but the situation really should have been spotted and dealt with earlier. The moral is: aggressive behaviour from other children must be highlighted to their parents or carers as soon as it is noticed, so that they can nip it in the bud. Don't be afraid to take action if you feel your child is being bullied in any way, shape or form.

MAKING MEAL TIMES FUN

'A child should always say what's true,
And speak when he is spoken to,
And behave mannerly at the table;
At least as far as he is able.'
– Whole Duty of Children, ROBERT LOUIS STEVENSON

Taking good care of children means feeding them well. We have already seen that you need to offer your toddler a wide variety of fresh organic fruits and vegetables, organic meats, free-range chicken and fish, wholemeal breads, pulses, grains, cheeses, eggs and yogurts – and the occasional treat thrown in for good measure.

When they reach two and a half, however, it sometimes seems as if a light switch is flicked off: they often suddenly stop eating and go off their food completely. Some toddlers may replace food with milk, some may eat so little you can hardly believe that they will survive. The fussy-eater stage is very normal at this age, and is mostly due to the fact that life has become so much more interesting. Sitting at the table seems a complete waste of exploring time – they would much rather be doing something else.

All you can do is try not to worry, and persevere by offering your toddler a wide variety of different, healthy, colourful and nutritious foods. Never force a child to eat. You will create a difficult pattern where your toddler will use not eating as a way of gaining power over you.

If you do find yourself getting worried about their eating habits, go back and read Tuck for Toddlers (page 61) to reassure yourself. Remember, toddlers will eat all their body requires – as little as that may seem to the grown-up eye. Their appetite does come back and balance out between the ages of three and four, but in the meantime you need to invent ways to make food fun. You can do that by being a bit creative and always involving your toddler in the meal-time process.

SITTING AT THE TABLE

Make place settings interesting

If your toddler adamantly refuses to sit at the table, you need to encourage and entice them by decorating their place setting with interesting objects. Novelty wipe-clean placemats with maps of the world, the alphabet, colours, wild animals, farm animals or sea creatures are fun to look at during the slow course of meal times, and they give you and your toddler something to talk about and learn from. I knew one little girl who memorised every king and queen of England from a placemat. Another little chap learned every European capital city from his. Help your toddler to arrange their own place setting and choose which dishes, cups or glasses they would like to place at their very own setting. You could even make your own placemat together.

MISS POPPY'S HOME-MADE PLACEMATS

You will need:

A 30cm x 40cm (12in x 16in) piece of card (construction paper)

Coloured markers

A roll of clear sticky-back plastic

Decorative bits: stickers, photographs, glitter, pieces of

Coloured foil cut up into squares, triangles, rectangles and stars

A stick of glue

Scissors

You can decorate both sides of the mat. I suggest that on one side you trace around a plate with a coloured marker. Do the same with a knife – even if your child is not using a knife yet – fork, spoon, cup or glass and napkin. That way your child will learn the simple plate setting and how to set the table. Let them decorate the other side of the card with a photograph of themselves or a favourite animal or pet. Stick on some shapes or letters of the alphabet for them to learn, sprinkle with glitter and generally have a bit of fun. Peel back the clear sticky-back plastic and cover one side generously. Turn the card over and repeat the process, trimming the sides neatly when you have finished. Voila! They now have their very own personalised placemat.

Molly my sister and I fell out
And what do you think it was all about?
She loved coffee and I loved tea
And that was the reason we couldn't agree!

There are lots of other ways of making meal times fun. Why not invite Teddy or other nursery guests and set them their very own place setting at the table? Nothing beats an audience, and your toddler can practice and perform some excellent table manners in front of them. Try placing a name card at each setting – they can easily be made with a piece of paper or cardboard, so why not cut out the back of a cereal box or use the rectangular lid? Let them draw and decorate their own name, or make a picture of their own design. Squiggly whirls of spaghetti, for example – how perfect for a place setting!

Choose a brightly coloured cloth napkin – if you don't have one look through your tea-towel drawer and see if you have something that will do instead. Napkin rings can be made by gluing a folded rectangular strip of paper into a circle, which your child can then colour in. You could also use a piece of coloured string, ribbon or rope. Old shower curtain rings work just as well, or you could make a trip to the shops and let your toddler choose a new napkin and a napkin ring for themselves.

Even picking a few wild flowers with your toddler and letting them place them in a vase at their place setting can excite them about meal times and make them want to sit at the table. Try collecting a few leaves and fallen acorns at the park and creating an autumnal table scene.

Let them dig through the kitchen drawers and cupboards and find a plate or dish, a spoon, a fork and a glass or cup they would

like to use. One little girl I knew insisted on drinking her milk from a sherry glass she found in her grandmother's drinks cabinet, and she handled it with very great care indeed. She also insisted on candlelight at each meal – including breakfast – and on eating her chicken soup with chopsticks, which took quite a while until she hit upon the idea of finishing it off with a ladle. As she was going through a fussy-eater stage, I didn't mind what she ate with – just as long as she ate! A family of four children I cared for told me that the spoons they used to eat their cornflakes at breakfast belonged to their great, great, great-aunt Anne Boleyn. They revelled in telling me that she last used one particular spoon just before she was beheaded – which normally brought chaos as each child pointed, guessed and teased each other as to who had the dreaded spoon that particular morning.

For special treats, meal times can be enjoyed as a picnic, either inside or out. Lay down a blanket or tablecloth and away you go. Lots of my charges have enjoyed eating inside their tents, and you can make an inside tent by throwing a sheet over a table or a few chairs scattered around. Some of them have made elaborate dens out of large cardboard boxes and, as a special treat, have eaten lunch or dinner inside. They have great fun which is, after all, what childhood should be all about.

MAKING FOOD FUN

Once you have your toddler sitting at the table, you need to get them to eat. If they are being particularly fussy, suggest they help devise a menu with you. Ask them their favourite colours of the day. If they choose red, green and yellow, tell them that they are only going to eat foods of that colour on that particular day. What could be more fun and nutritious than popping raw peas out of the pod when they are nice and crunchy? Try some red tomato sauce with green or yellow pasta. Green apples, red raspberries and melon-yellow yogurt all make for a delicious dessert. You could give them red cranberry juice or yellow pineapple juice to drink – don't forget to water all juices down. You'll be amazed at what you can come up with. If you are lucky enough to have a garden to grow food in, go and explore what red, green and yellow foods you can find that might be ripe and fresh to eat. A trip to your local farmers' market or supermarket can add a whole adventure to the day, or even better would be a farm where you can pick your own produce – apples or strawberries or yellow corn perhaps.

Teach children where food comes from It is so important in this age of processed and fast foods that we teach children where their food actually comes from. In a perfect world, all schools would have their own vegetable garden and fruit orchard. Children will eat anything they have grown themselves, and absolutely love to pick their own vegetables and fruits. Nothing beats pulling carrots from the ground like Peter Rabbit, or picking fresh blackberries from a bush and bringing them home to eat with stained-black fingertips and lips to match.

Do you carrot all for me?
My heart beets for you
With your turnip nose
And your radish face
You are a peach
If we cantaloupe
Lettuce marry
Weed make a swell pear

Children love to be involved in preparing their own foods and decorating them, and you will find that they are much more eager to try new foods this way. Use different-shaped pastry-cutters to cut out fun shapes and designs. Be imaginative, and think hors d'oeuvre size: blini-style pancakes spread with mashed avocado, a

small piece of cheese and a peeled grape on top. Food should be made to look as attractive as possible to children, and this is especially true of healthy foods. Why do you think all children crave visits to the fast-food restaurants? It is mostly because of the colourful packaging and free toy – that and the fact that they drench their foods in sugar and salt. If you take your toddler to the supermarket and give them free range to choose what they would like, they will always choose the foods in the most colourful, garish packaging. I often wonder why they don't market healthy foods in the same way.

MISS POPPY'S FUN FOOD SUGGESTIONS

HEALTHY FOOD PARCEL

Save a fast-food hamburger box, give it a good wash and serve a healthy meal of home-made fresh salmon nuggets, fresh garden peas and brown rice. Add little extras like a toothpick to stab the peas, or a small wooden or plastic spoon like the ones you used to get stuck to the top of ice-cream pots. Fix them to the top of the fast-food packet so your toddler has a little parcel to open. For the fresh salmon nuggets you will need:

125g (5oz) fresh salmon fillet, any remaining bones removed
3 tablespoons plain flour
fresh breadcrumbs
1 tablespoon rolled oats
1 teaspoon finely chopped fresh parsley
1 egg, beaten
olive oil

Cut the fish into 2cm (1in) strips and roll in the flour. Set aside. Mix the breadcrumbs with the rolled oats and the parsley. Dip the fish into the egg and then roll in the breadcrumb mixture. Cover and place in the fridge for 20–30 minutes. Sprinkle with olive oil and bake at 200°C/400°F/Gas Mark 6 for 12–15 minutes until golden crisp.

CHINESE MEAL

Fill up a Chinese takeaway box with healthy noodles, cooked according to the instructions on the packet and tossed in a little sunflower oil, some sesame oil and sesame seeds. Offer a pair of chopsticks for authenticity and an extra giggle. Serve a fortune fruit rather than a fortune cookie for dessert. Cut an apple in half and scoop out the middle core to create room for a little message. Put a tiny piece of paper in the middle with a sweet little message or just a smiley face, sandwich the apple back together and tie it up with a ribbon or a piece of string.

KIDDY DIPS

Serving dinner on an unusual plate is an excellent way of keeping your child interested in their food. Try one of those long rectangular plates with small indentations for different types of olive. Fill up each dent with separate foods such as cherry tomatoes, bite-size home-made chicken nuggets (made just like the fresh salmon nuggets on page 187, but you will need to cook them for 20–25 minutes), small florets of broccoli, chunks of pineapple and cheese. Think colour, size and nutritional value. You could also make a hummus dip by mashing up some chickpeas, or a healthy raita by

mixing plain Greek yogurt with chopped cucumber and dried apricots. Make little kebabs by grilling small, bite-size pieces of salmon, chicken or meat and placing them around the side of the dish. You can also add a mini skewer of raw vegetables, cubes of cucumber, celery, carrot, yellow peppers and cherry tomatoes. For dessert make mini fruit skewers from chunks of watermelon, apple, banana, kiwi and berries. Offer fruit yogurt as a dip.

NOVELTY POTS

Save attractive novelty yogurt pots and use them to serve a meal – a pot of raw carrot and cucumber sticks, or lightly cooked green beans or asparagus sticks, a pot of pasta in fresh tomato sauce, a pot of grated cheese and a pot of bite-size meatballs. Or you could serve a few healthy snacks like raisins, cubes of cheese, peeled grapes or cubes of cooked tofu in a cupcake case to make them more attractive. As a special treat serve fresh fruit with a dollop of fromage frais or frozen yogurt in an ice-cream wafer cup.

TACOS

Tacos shells can be filled with all sorts of food. Fill small dishes with various foods for your toddler to fill their own shell. You could try shredded lettuce, cabbage or spinach leaves, mince cooked with onions, shredded chicken, turkey, thin slices of beef, grated carrot, courgettes (zucchini), thinly sliced sticks of red, yellow, green or orange peppers, grated cheese, tofu, red kidney beans or black beans – the list is almost endless. Add a few dips such as hummus, yogurt or mashed avocado and tomato.

SUSHI ROLLS

Make-your-own sushi kits are readily available in health-food shops and supermarkets, and they are great fun to make. Many toddlers like smoked salmon, but it can easily be replaced with vegetables, tofu, ham, chicken, meat or poached salmon.

TABLE MANNERS

I believe that a well-fed child is a well-behaved child, but there are certain table manners I expect from an older toddler of three to four years:

>   Always wash hands before meal times
>   Help to set and clear the table
>   No screaming, shouting or yelling at the table
>   No throwing food
>   No fighting with other siblings
>   Always say 'please' and 'thank you'

Always start meal times with good general hygiene. All little – and big – hands should be washed before you start preparing, playing with and eating food. I have a collection of plastic bugs and I always pop one on to each child's plate before the food is served as a fun reminder for them to wash their hands – otherwise creepy bugs can crawl into their food, into their mouths, down their throats and into stinky tummy bugs. The children duly hand me back the bugs, proud of the fact that they have remembered to wash their hands.

Remove a naughty child from the table

The only way to deal with naughtiness at the table is to remove your toddler from their food. Place them in another room or just away from the table, get down to their level, look them straight in the eye and in a firm, clear manner explain that their behaviour is not acceptable. Tell them they may return to the table in a few minutes when all the naughtiness has ended, and then give them a second chance to return and finish their food. If another sibling is teasing or taunting them, remove the other sibling and repeat the same procedure as before. If the pattern of behaviour continues, just end the meal time, and make it clear that they will not be having any pudding. Stick firm to your decision despite all the begging and pleading. Make it clear that naughtiness at the table is not acceptable and will not be tolerated. Once they realise there's no dessert if they are naughty, the matter is usually sorted out fairly quickly.

Sometimes their behaviour is not really their fault. They may have a guest over who exhibits the most awful table manners which your toddler will of course absolutely adore and want to copy. There is nothing much you can do here, as it's not really fair to tell an unfamiliar child off in front of their friend, especially when they are on strange territory. This will only humiliate them and embarrass your child. The best thing to do is try to let it pass this once, or make a joke out of it – 'Joshua, I had no idea you learned your table manners at the zoo!' Get them on your side and then suggest there be a prize for the best table manners. Just watch them whip into shape. If your toddler continues to copy their bad example when they have long gone, repeat the same technique as before – remove them from the table until they are ready to behave properly.

Teach your toddler to excuse themselves from the table by paying attention and noticing when they have finished. Gently remind them to say, 'Thank you. Please may I leave the table?' A simple 'Excuse me' or 'Thank you' will do nicely for the younger child. If you encourage this from an early age it will soon enough become a very good habit.

Bon appetit!

GOOD NIGHT, SLEEP TIGHT

'And does it not seem hard to you,
When all the sky is clear and blue,
And I should like so much to play,
To have to go to bed by day?'
– *Bed in Summer,* ROBERT LOUIS STEVENSON

Sweet Sayings to Share at Bedtime:

'See you in the morning, when the day is dawning'
'Sleep tight, wake bright'
'The longer you sleep, the longer you'll grow'
'Time to blow out the moon'
[Switch off the main light as they blow]
'Good night, sleep tight, don't let the bed bugs bite'
'Up the wooden hill and down sheet lane'
'Good night
Sweet repose
Lie on your back
And not your nose'

Keep bedtime the same every night

Hopefully by now you will have established an exceedingly good bedtime routine. If you are still having difficulty, go back and read Sweet Dreams (page 98). It will offer you comfort and support, good tips and ideas on how to help you re-establish your bedtime routine. Remember to try to be consistent and keep bedtime the same time every night. If you have recently moved house or have been away on holiday, the routine may be a bit scattered, but it shouldn't be too problematic to whip it back into shape once you are back on familiar territory. Be firm: your toddler will now be much more vocal and verbal, and able to dictate. Give yourself a week to re-establish your routine, and don't give up!

You may notice that as your toddler gets older, they find it harder to wind down at the end of a busy day's activities, especially once they start a playgroup or preschool. The social interaction, the excitement, the new games to learn, the whole business of having to adjust and fit in – all of these are physically and mentally exhausting for your toddler. This is why naps are still a crucial part of their daytime routine. A nap will refresh them enough to be able to cope with the rest of the day's activities and prevent major meltdowns over seemingly minor issues. As you may have grasped, I am a great believer in naps, and in keeping them as long as you can. Experience has taught me that the more sleep a child has, the more relaxed they are, and the more relaxed you are. So keeping their naps longer benefits everyone.

By the time your toddler reaches three or four, however, you will probably find that they start to grow out of their naps. You'll be pleased to know that Miss Poppy has a solution. It's called 'quiet time'. As they get older, it will evolve into reading time. All my charges have been voracious readers, and I'm convinced it was partly due to the evolution of quiet time into reading time.

Quiet time is time your toddler spends alone in their room sitting peacefully on their bed or floor looking at their books. The objective is to invite sleep and encourage it, but never to mention it. If the dreaded word 'sleep' creeps into the conversation, you will be greeted with fits of refusal. So, as soon as lunch is over, explain to your toddler that it is now quiet time. Pop them in their bedroom and settle them down with a few good books to look at while you explain to them what the plan for the afternoon is – something for them to look forward to in order to make them realise that there is life after quiet time.

Once they are settled, don't dilly-dally! Don't be persuaded to read the books to them, or get into a lengthy conversation with them. Explain that this is their time to be alone and to relax for a little while. Often you will find they drop off to sleep in a matter of ten or fifteen minutes, which is excellent but not imperative – the object is to give them time alone to relax without any attention focused upon them and with no expectations. Learning to be alone and to enjoy their own company is a wonderful thing to teach children.

Quiet time means being alone

You have to be persistent with quiet time, and don't expect them to stay in their rooms for too long at the beginning. Aim for fifteen to twenty minutes at first and you will find that it will become naturally longer once they learn to involve themselves and enjoy the pleasure of their books. If they keep on tottering out of their room, just pop them straight back in and explain that quiet time is not over yet. If they are reluctant to go back and read their books, I have found that audio books come in very handy. If you have a cassette machine or CD player, set it up in their room for use during quiet time. There are many wonderful stories on audio book, often told in fabulously animated ways to capture the child's interest. Always stick to a story tape during quiet time rather than any interactive music tapes – your objective is to keep them still rather than have them up and dancing. Your child may kick up a fuss about being on the bed, preferring instead to lie on the floor to look at their books. If so, create a cosy little sleeping area – even a little tent – with a pillow and a blanket or sleeping bag. Let Teddy snuggle in and, with a bit of luck, they will have all dozed off for a nap before the end of the story tape. Keep noises and distractions to a minimum during quiet time. Sometimes they ask you to leave their bedroom door open, which is fine as long as it is quiet in the rest of the house.

If they do fall asleep during quiet time, an hour and a half to two hours is a sufficient period to let them sleep. Try not to let them go beyond two hours or else it will cut into their afternoon's activity time. When you do wake them up, be very gentle. Talk softly, stroke their backs and offer them a sip of water or juice. Give them a good fifteen to twenty minutes to adjust as they will be slightly disorientated and will often cry. Give them a big cuddle, comfort them and start to discuss your afternoon plans.

There are so many great benefits to encouraging and nurturing quiet time, but you do have to be persistent as it does not happen immediately. It's worth it, though, as your toddler will be so much happier and more cooperative after a rest – so if at first you don't succeed, try and try again.

BAD DREAMS

'A ruffled mind makes a restless pillow.'
– The Professor, CHARLOTTE BRONTE

As your toddler grows, they will become more active in society. Attending playgroups, preschool or music groups are big steps for your little one – they become physically separated from you and experience peer pressure for the first time. So much is changing, and this can cause them anxiety. One way in which this manifests itself is sleepless nights.

Bad dreams are fairly common between the ages of three and four because children of this age have a very active imagination. They can be of varying degrees – you may well find yourself woken in the night by a sudden scream or yelp and rush into their bedroom only to find that they are still fast asleep. Often, though, they will come and find you, and it is very important that you physically comfort and cuddle them. It is best to take them back into their own bedroom to do this, however, so that they can feel comforted in their own space. You can stop them feeling scared about being in their bedroom by making sure the night light is on and leaving their door ajar with the landing light on. Often they will ask to sleep with you in your bed after a bad dream, which is fine if it's once in a blue moon. If it develops into an unhealthy habit of them arriving in your bed every night, you need to take action and return them to their own bed so you all have a good night's sleep.

Too much horseplay or excitement before bedtime can also lead to a disrupted night's sleep. It's best to keep the activities calm, uncompetitive and relaxed just before bedtime. Physical play can lead to over-excitement which can in turn lead to tears, and the last thing you want at the end of the day is for your child to go to bed unhappy. You yourself know that if you go to bed worried or upset it's much harder to relax and fall into a deep sleep. A parent's arrival home from work is often a cause for great excitement – as indeed it should be – but best to wind down together as quickly as you can. Give your child your undivided attention, remain peaceful and calm and just enjoy being in the same room together. Avoid any complicated projects or physical activities.

Sam, Sam the butcher man
Washed his face in a frying pan
Combed his hair with a wagon wheel
And died with a toothache in his heel

BEDWETTING

Bedwetting is fairly common: one in ten children still wet their bed up until the age of eight years old. In many cases it is believed to be hereditary, so if you or your partner had difficulty staying dry throughout the night, I'm afraid there's a chance that your offspring will too. However, it is also often caused by emotional factors triggered by changes in environment: starting school, changes in family structures, a new baby, parents' separation or a new marriage. It could be something much more simple, such as your child not being confident finding their way to the bathroom at night. This can be helped by making sure there is a well-lit hallway and a night light in their bedroom and the bathroom. I once discovered that a charge of mine was scared of the shadow of a big old oak tree blustering in the wind at night against the bathroom window. This was resolved by placing a blind up against the window and putting a strong night light in the bathroom. Don't get upset if they wake you in the middle of the night to ask you to take them to the toilet in a strange and unfamiliar place such as a new house or in a hotel or when visiting friends or relatives.

I believe that bedwetting problems are often down to the reaction of the parent or carer. The more you react negatively, the worse they will feel about it and the more the cycle is likely to continue. Of course, it is hard to be faced with a wet child and a wet bed every morning, but try not to make a fuss about it. Mention it, but in a way that makes them feel less as though they are to blame – 'Oh dear, wet again! We must try to do something about it.' 'We' is important. It shares the problem and makes the child feel less alone.

Don't get too upset about bedwetting

There are various things you can do to try and break the cycle of bedwetting. Restart the process of night-time lifting: before you go to bed, simply wake your child and walk them to the toilet, sitting with them until they go. You can also start using nappies again at night, but be prepared for the fact that they may dislike this intensely as they associate it with babies. Restrict fluids for an hour before bedtime, and keep this up for a good two weeks. Don't mention to them what you are doing, but keep a note of any dry nappies when they wake up with. Praise them if they are dry; say nothing if they are wet. After you have had three or four dry nappies in a row, try a night without a nappy. Don't make a big deal about it before they go to bed, but if they wake up dry, do make a big deal about that. Continue with this pattern of praising dryness but saying nothing at wetness.

Please do not worry about bedwetting: it is perfectly normal. Older children can become embarrassed about it, especially if they are invited to spend the night at their friends and are worried about wetting the bed. Sometimes this works as an incentive to stay dry, but just in case, mention it to the friend's parents or carer in advance and in private, and ask that they wake your child before they go to bed and take them to the toilet. Also mention it might be wise to cut down on the amount of drinks they offer before bedtime. Reassure your child in advance that their friend's parents will know how to take care of them and this will relieve some of their anxiety and help them relax and have a better time.

Finally, remember to keep a waterproof covering over the mattress, and sprinkle it with lavender oil to keep a fresh smell.

MISS POPPY'S GUIDE TO CHILDCARE

Childcare is an issue that most parents – and certainly all working parents – will need to tackle at some stage in their child's development. It can be an emotive subject, as leaving your child in the care of somebody else when you have been used to being with them all day every day can be immensely difficult. But my experience is that most children benefit hugely from being placed in a stimulating environment away from their parents, even if it is only for a couple of mornings a week.

Of course, all children are different, as are all parents. When you decide to start taking advantage of the various forms of childcare depends on a number of factors, such as your confidence, your child's confidence or the needs of working parents to have somebody to look after their child while they bring home the bacon. Some parents will decide to start sending their child to nursery or to day care, or to enlist the help of a nanny, as early as six months, which is absolutely fine. It is at around the age of two and a half years, however, that most parents decide to start using some form of childcare.

Finding the right childcare to fit your specific needs can seem a bit daunting for parents. The good news is that there is a wide range of options available. Your choices will of course depend upon your personal and financial situation, but the key thing for you to consider is whether you want your child to be cared for in their own home, or whether you want them to be exposed to other children and environments. All of these options come with pros and cons, but what is certain is that creating a stable environment for your child to feel nurtured, cared for and stimulated takes a lot of hard work from all concerned.

NURSERIES

By the age of two and a half years, your toddler may be ready for two or three mornings a week of structured play at a nursery school. It offers them the chance to function in a group situation and develop their social skills. They will practise sharing, taking turns and making friends which all lead to kindness and an understanding of others. The teacher, you will find, will impress your child enormously, and their authority will have a huge influence on them. Many a time I have rather sneakily suggested to a three-year-old that their teacher loves spinach and going to bed at night!

There are many different types of nursery. The best way to choose a suitable nursery school is to visit as many as you can in your area to observe the environment and see if it suits the personality of your child. If you are placing your young baby in a nursery, you need to observe how other the babies are cared for. Are there enough members of staff, and what are their qualifications with babies? Are they hired solely to care for the babies, or are they also expected to care for the elder children? What is their appearance like, and do they have a high level of personal hygiene? Are the babies allowed to follow a routine as far as feeding goes, or are they fed on demand? Ask to see the changing areas and check that they are clean. How long are they left just sitting in their chair or cot, and how often are they physically picked up, cuddled and played with? Does their environment change or are they left to remain in one particular area of the nursery all day? How much fresh air are they exposed to? How is illness handled? Is there a doctor or registered nurse on call throughout the day for emergencies? Babies need a lot of care. Look around the nursery and see if it is being provided.

Take plenty of time to check out different nurseries

Although you will be probably be shown around by the nursery manager, try to meet and interact with the rest of the staff. Do you

like them? Are they friendly, chatty and approachable? Are they affectionate with the children? How do they handle conflict with the children when it arises? Are their opinions on discipline and general childcare the same as yours, or do they differ? Does the nursery have one clear, common policy on childcare, or does it seem to vary between each member of staff? Do they welcome *Spend time* input with you, and an open dialogue about your child? Look for *with the staff* fun, optimistic, kind and understanding teachers with an ability to discipline through teaching and learning. A good teacher will closely observe without interfering with a child's play, and divert conflict before it has a chance to escalate.

Find out about cost and flexibility – what happens if you arrive early or late, and what about sick days? Is there a sickbay, or is it recommended the parents collect the child and care for them at home?

There are certain things to look for in a classroom, but by far the most important of these is happy, busy children. Do they look stimulated? Are they interacting with other children and staff? Do they seem clean, healthy and well cared for? Are they separated into groups concentrating on one activity at a time, or are they allowed to wander freely from one activity to another? Is there a routine or schedule to the activities of the day such as meals, snacks, naps, outdoor play, sports, arts and crafts, reading, music and dance?

Arrange visits around lunchtime so that you can see what sort of food is served. Ask about special diets and allergies – how closely are they followed and monitored for each child? Is there a varied selection of healthy, well-balanced, nutritious foods on offer? What about snacks and drinks served throughout the rest of the day? Are children encouraged to brush their teeth after eating?

Walk around and check out the premises fully, both indoor and out. Pay special attention to the bathrooms and sleeping areas. Are the walls painted and decorated with artwork or educational images such as the alphabet or numbers? Are the mats clean and comfy? Is the floor area kept neat and orderly? Is it carpeted for comfy crawling, or tiled? Are the blankets or duvets washed regularly, or do you have to provide them from home? Are the play areas adequately equipped with toys, books, puzzles, games and art-and-craft supplies? There should be separate play areas. A quiet rug or carpeted area with well-stocked bookshelves is important for relaxing and reading. There should be a pretend play area, perhaps with a pretend kitchen with utensils and dressing-up clothes and props. Some nurseries have a water or sand area with digging and pouring utensils and waterproof aprons. Most have a painting area with easels, paper and pots of paint, and an outside or indoor open space with climbing equipment, balls, bicycles, trucks and cars to drive around so that they can get some good exercise. Classrooms often have a pet goldfish or hamster who will be greatly coveted and all the children will want to look after it during the school holidays. Before you leave, ask for the names and telephone numbers of other parents so that you can call and ask for a reference.

You may find – and this is especially true if your child is starting preschool at the age of three and a half and has never attended a playgroup or nursery school before – that they are reluctant to be separated from you. This is perfectly normal. Many children go through this stage and it is considered normal development, so do not worry about it. There are ways to ease and smooth the transition which will help your child settle in. Always visit the nursery with your child at least twice before you leave them there. Most good nurseries will offer you the chance to spend the morning there with your child as an introduction to starting school. Take their hand and lead them around the classroom, showing them the different areas for play. Show them the lockers or cubby holes where they put their coats. Most importantly, show them where the bathroom is and make sure they know their way back to class.

If your child is lucky enough to have a sibling at the same school, you will find it easier as they are likely to be familiar with the environment. Often the younger sibling can't wait to attend proper school and runs into the classroom at any given opportunity. If this is not the case, though, your child will need a chance to meet the teacher in the environment where he or she will become familiar – the classroom – and get to know the other children who will be in their class. Try to invite one or two over separately for tea and playtime so that they can develop a friendship before school actually begins. Ask the teacher for a class list which will have the names and telephone numbers of each member of the class.

Some children like to take a teddy or a toy that reminds them of home. This may or may not be allowed, depending on the school rules. Ask the teacher – maybe they can keep it in their locker for safe keeping. Often children are allowed to bring a photograph of themselves or of the whole family to stick on their locker. This can offer great reassurance throughout the morning – you can even give them a small photograph of yourself to keep in their pocket so that they can still feel close to you. One little chap I cared for had a locket with two tiny photographs of his parents – which he proudly displayed to the class. It offered him great comfort throughout the morning.

Enlist the teacher's help

If your child does begin to get upset when you leave, ask the teacher for assistance. Often they can be distracted by a particular toy or by reading a story together. More often than not, the tears suddenly disappear as soon as you are out of sight. It's important for you to remain strong and try not to be anxious; if you are, your child will pick up on it. Stay positive and calm when saying goodbye, and keep it quick and precise. As soon as they busy themselves with something, off you go. Then it's time for you to busy yourself with something so you don't get upset or feel abandoned. Before you know it, two or three hours will have passed and it will be time to pick them up again.

Don't be surprised if your child has a tantrum of some sort when they see you. Mostly it will be a result of them feeling comfortable enough to let it all out and express themselves after a busy morning spent learning, adjusting and trying to fit in – the fact that they know how you are going to react means that you offer some comfort in their changing world. It's nothing a little nap or an hour of quiet time won't sort out.

A final word of advice: you may find that your child's behaviour deteriorates when they start nursery. They might just become a bit more difficult, or more demanding of your attention. Sometimes they start acting rather babyish. This is perfectly normal. Children often regress slightly when they are mastering – and excelling – at something else, and starting nursery school is a big moment for them. You just need to be patient: this stage will soon pass.

CHILDMINDERS (DAY CARE)

Registered childminders are experienced, self-employed childcare providers – often mothers themselves – who look after other people's children at home. You should always check that a childminder you are considering using is registered. In order to be registered, the childminder will have undergone a personal interview and had their home checked for suitability and safety. They and anyone else in the house over the age of sixteen will also have undergone a police check. Childminders are generally allowed to care for a maximum of six children – three under-fives and three between the ages of five and eight – and that number includes any children of their own. Rates vary depending on where you live.

It is important to visit as many childminders as you can find in your area so you can get a good sense of what is available and how they differ. A good childminder will probably have a waiting list, but it's worth going to see them nevertheless, if only to understand why. Visit while the childminder is on duty with her charges so that you can watch how she interacts with the children, and also so that you can meet them. Look to see if the children seem happy, busy and stimulated. Don't be afraid to ask as many questions as you like, such as:

How do they handle discipline?

Are meals included, and if so what are they?

Do they offer healthy snacks? are they served at regular intervals or available all day? What about sweets?

Can you send a packed lunch, or some home-made foods?

What are their views on tv? How much television are the children exposed to during the day?

Is the day structured into some sort of routine? If so, what is it? Can they give you an example of a regular day?

What sort of arts and crafts do they do?

Does the childminder read to the children?

If your child has a routine, is the childminder prepared to follow it?

Is there a separate sleeping area?

What would they do if your child became ill while in their care?

Are you informed in advance if the other children are sick so that you can decide whether or not you want your child exposed to any illness?

Are the hours flexible?

What is the price? Does it include food, nappies and anything else your child needs during the day?

What do you have to provide as far as equipment goes? You might have to take bottles, nappies, extra clothing, bedding, a buggy or a car seat

Ask for a tour of the premises and pay close attention to the number of toys, puzzles, books and games that are provided. Look for child-size furniture. Is there any art-and-craft work visibly displayed around the house? Is there an outside play area for fresh air and a space to run around in? If not, are the children taken to the local park or playground, and what method of transport do they use to get there with a handful of youngsters. If they are driving, check to see that they have enough car seats and that they are in full working order. Ask about their driving-licence record. Check for all-round cleanliness and general safety – there should be safety gates, cupboards should have locks on them, all fires should be covered with a fireguard and electric sockets should be fitted with childproof covers. What are the bathroom facilities like? Is there a changing area and a stool so small children can safely climb on to the toilet by themselves and reach the sink to wash their hands? Does the childminder smoke? If there are likely to be any other adults in the house during the day, ask to meet them and vet them thoroughly. Check to see if there are animals in the house and how they are cared for. Ask about the children's safety if she allows the animal to roam freely around the house.

If you are satisfied, suggest bringing your child around for the second interview. Pay close attention to how the childminder interacts with your child and determine how curious they are by the number of questions they ask about them and their personality. *Watch your child with the childminders* Communication is key here. You need to be able to talk to her and discuss your child in detail, and vice versa. Follow your instincts, but also ask to speak to the parents of the other children she cares for to get a reference. Professional childminders will be more than happy to oblige.

NANNIES

People have so many preconceptions about nannies, most of which are derived from Mary Poppins, The Sound of Music and, unfortunately, The Hand that Rocks the Cradle. Well, let's get a few things straight: we do not fly high in the sky, unless we are in a 747; we tend not to be failed nuns with fine voices who are after your husband; and generally speaking, we are not psychotic, manic-depressive murderers!

Nannies are trained, qualified childcarers. They are predominantly female but there are now male nannies – or 'mannies' – graduating from different childcare courses around the country. They can be live-in or live-out, and they take care of all your children's basic needs, as well as looking after their belongings, bedrooms, clothes and toys, and doing their washing, ironing and sewing. Most nannies shop and cook for their charges, and organise their activities and general social life. Some nannies share the childcare with the parents, others take full responsibility for it.

Throughout my career I have met an abundance of wonderful nannies who have devoted their lives to raising other people's children. Many have given up the opportunity of having their own family for the sake of their charges, and so they stay with them, nurturing, caring and loving them just as if they were their own children. Many stay until the child is old enough to head off to college or university. To me, the relationship between a nanny and her charge is a true love story, a story of devotion, caring day in day out and getting through the difficult years – yes, years! Many nannies never get the recognition they deserve, but at the end of the day they see a decent, loving, kind and understanding human being all ready for the big wide world. The knowledge that they have helped raise that person is reward enough.

If you manage to find one of these nannies, hold on tight to her – she will be in great demand. Most nannies stay for a maximum of four years, as they often specialise in looking after children of certain ages. Some excel with newborns but struggle with challenging, inquisitive, physically active four-year-olds. I have seen many nannies in action, and the best of them are able to adapt to new situations: they listen, watch and observe their new family and charge, and then use their own childcare experience to fit in with what they have seen.

Nannies are probably the most expensive type of childcare, but their salaries do differ according to their qualifications, age and experience. Where you live – city rates are normally higher – and how many children the nanny will be caring for are also factors. Live-in nannies will need their own separate bedroom and access to a bathroom, which can be shared with the children. If you live in a rural area, access to a car should be provided for when she is both on and off duty. You should discuss in advance what you will pay her for any extra work in the evenings and weekends.

I always tell parents that finding the right nanny is rather like dating: you keep going until you find the right one for you. Of course, if you find the right nanny you should keep her as long as you can in order to offer your child as much continuity as possible. At the same time, my feeling is that it is better to have a good nanny for one year than a bad nanny for ten.

There are a number of professional qualifications for nannies, and you should ensure that anybody you are thinking of employing has one of these. However you go about finding a nanny, you must be prepared to spend quite a bit of effort and time sifting and sorting through CVs in order to pick out the best candidates to interview. You will also need to do extensive background searches and reference checks on your selected candidates. If all this sounds like far too much work, you can go to a nanny agency. If it's a good one, the agency should have thoroughly researched all the candidates before they send them to you for an interview. They will have interviewed you thoroughly to determine what your individual childcare needs are, and clearly explained what you should expect to pay and what is included in the cost. Of course, nanny agencies vary in their quality, so it is a good idea to ask other parents if they have used an agency they can recommend. It is also worth asking your friends' nannies if they can recommend anybody – they are likely to be clued up as to the local situation. But whatever you do, don't ask your friend's nanny to be your nanny – it's a sure way to end a friendship fast!

Before you employ a nanny, you will need to give her a thorough interview. You need to be sure that they have the same views on raising children as you do. It can be very hard to make a sound judgement from a single interview, but if you ask the right questions and are on the lookout, you can learn a lot during that first hour. Make a list of topics you want to discuss and questions you want to ask. These might include:

> What are her qualifications and experience?
> How does she handle discipline?

Is she used to working with a parent who stays at home?

Is she used to working alone?

How flexible is she? Would she be able to work the
occasional weekend?

How would she react to you being late home from work?

What is her diet like? is she healthy and well versed on nutrition?

What activities does she think are suitable for your age child?

What are her views on children watching TV?

How would she describe an average day with a charge?

How would she spend the school holidays? what activities would
she recommend?

Can she drive, and does she have a clean driving licence?

How would she handle a medical emergency?

How does she feel about travelling together with you as a family
on holiday?

If she's a live-out nanny, how would she feel about occasionally
sleeping over?

If she's a live-in nanny, what are her feelings about both your
and her privacy?

During the interview, watch how she interacts with you child. Is
she responsive, and is your child responsive to her? Ask her about
herself and her past jobs. Listen carefully to how she talks about
her previous employer. If she is negative and complains about her
past experiences, beware. Don't be afraid to say what it is you are
looking for in a nanny and ask her if she's up to the job. If you are
interviewing for a live-in nanny, show her the room and bathroom
you are intending to provide. Discuss privacy issues. For example,
do you want your nanny hanging around eating dinner with you
every night, or would you prefer that she made herself scarce after
hours? If so, you need to provide her with a TV and telephone in
her bedroom so that she is more self-sufficient, and you will need
to discuss what times she can use the kitchen at night. Do you feel

comfortable with her having friends or boyfriends over? These might seem like small points, but it is essential to get them clarified at the beginning.

Weekends can be difficult times for live-in nannies, as often the child gets confused, does not understand it's nanny's day off and wanders into her room wanting to play. A good nanny understands this and will play with the child for a short while before returning them to their parents. (The child, of course, may be totally oblivious to this, and needs to be made to understand that however much the nanny loves them all, she needs her privacy.) By the same token, most families don't appreciate a nanny hanging around the house the whole weekend when it's their time with the children. A balance needs to be struck whereby you respect each other's boundaries.

For live-out nannies, you will need to be clear about definite morning start times and evening finish times, although both of you must be prepared for some flexibility. Remember that both you, the child and the nanny are sometimes ill or come across unforeseen circumstances.

The second interview should not be held until you have checked out her references. Don't be afraid to ask her former employer as many questions as you can think of. You need to know about your prospective nanny's sense of responsibility, punctuality, communication skills and flexibility. It is important that you ask how she handles conflict with both you and the children. Most former employers are more than happy to help and speak quite openly and honestly. It is also good to remember that all people are different and what may not have suited them suits you just fine, so keep an open mind and remember that relationships take a lot of time and effort to grow. Nothing is perfect, but most problems can be solved as long as the communication channels remain open.

Invite the nanny to spend a day with you

For the second interview, I recommend you invite the nanny to spend the whole day with you, and you should offer to give her a day's pay and travel expenses for this. It will be an invaluable way for her to get to know the children a bit better, and for you to get to know her. Try to let her spend as much time with the children as possible and allow her the freedom to set limits and deal with conflict if it arises. You will have a much clearer view after one whole day together, and this will help you to make your final decision.

It will be a big adjustment for all of you having a new nanny, especially if she is your first one. Working with someone in your home is very different to working with someone in an office. In an office situation, boundaries are clearly defined; in a private home they are less distinct. It is very important to be aware of this and maintain a well-mannered, courteous attitude towards each other – even when you do not feel like it. Do not confuse your personal and your professional relationship: you may find too much shared personal information shifts the balance of power and the distinction between employer and employee becomes blurred.

It would be useful for both of you if you spend at least one full week working side by side with your nanny, introducing her to your daily routines and schedules. I find it helpful to have a new notebook for each job, one that fits neatly into your pocket and can be used to jot down any important information. Give one to your nanny with a list of emergency contact numbers – a copy of which should also be hung next to the telephone – and any other information that you think she might need.

Introduce her to key people

If your child is going to school, it is important your nanny is introduced to the teacher and fellow parents and nannies. You may also want to introduce your nanny to your child's doctor and dentist. If you have family relatives and close friends nearby who are frequently involved with your children, make those introductions too, even if only by telephone. Some parents like their nanny to keep a daily diary where she can jot down any information – sleeping times, nappy times, eating times, new likes and dislikes and any upsets or problems. Diaries are a great way of sharing the day with a working parent, who will very much appreciate the nanny's effort and feel more in touch with their child.

Nannies should be provided with petty cash, along with a notebook to keep track of all expenditures and receipts. A nanny should never be out of pocket to an employer. She should also be given a mobile telephone so that you can always reach her and vice versa. She may already have her own mobile, so you might offer to pay a percentage of her bill if she allows it to be used for work purposes, or she could simply bill you for certain work-related calls.

Be very clear about your opinions on television and telephone usage while the nanny is on duty. Suggest she make her private phone calls during the child's nap times or when they are at school. Ask her what she likes to eat so that you can provide it. Invite her to take an hour for lunch, preferably while the child is sleeping or at school. Discuss if you have a preference as to which days you like your child's sheets to be changed and their bedroom thoroughly cleaned. If you have a separate cleaner, introduce them to the nanny and make sure it is very clear who cleans what. You might offer that the cleaner cleans the nanny's bedroom, or she may prefer to do it herself. All of these things may seem trivial, but slight things can lead to miscommunication and conflict, so it is much better to be clear from the beginning.

You need to be able to talk to your nanny about sensitive subjects without her feeling defensive and threatening to leave; equally, your nanny needs to be able to talk to you without resentment or anger and fear of being fired. This takes a lot of communication which should improve throughout your relationship. I recommend that once every two weeks you both sit down for a half-hour chat when you air your appreciation or highlight any grievances which have been brewing and try to sort them out calmly and fairly. Remember that all relationships take work, and this one is no different. Don't be hurt or take it as an insult if your nanny has any complaints: it's a job to her, not her life, so she may treat it with much less sensitivity than you would. If she gets defensive when you suggest how things might be done differently, make sure you highlight the positive aspects of what she is doing to make her feel more secure.

Make a time for regular chats

Good nannies are worth their weight in gold. Remember that, and show your appreciation every once in a while by writing her a card or giving her the occasional bunch of flowers. Always invite her along to your child's birthdays parties, as well as christenings and school events. Remember that she too is a part of your child's life.

MOTHERS' HELPS

A mothers' help is unqualified in formal childcare, although she is usually quite experienced, but she will assist you with household duties such as washing, ironing and general cleaning. Nannies, on the other hand, only do the children's housework. Like a nanny, mothers' helps can live in or out, but they are usually less expensive. The procedure for finding a good mothers' help is very like finding a nanny, although you will probably find you have a lot more applicants and will therefore need to be more selective and thorough in your reference-checking.

AU PAIRS

An au pair is a young foreign person who wishes to learn English in return for board, accommodation and a small allowance. They will babysit your children and help with general household chores for five to six hours a day, but must work no more than twenty-five hours in total a week, and will generally not work weekends. An au pair will usually attend a language school for half the day, and it is important to remember that au pairs are usually not experienced with children and they should therefore not be left in charge on their own.

An au pair should be treated like a member of your own family. Most of the time you will not have personally met your au pair before they arrive in the country; their details, along with a photograph, will have been sent for you to look over, and I suggest a telephone conversation or two before they arrive. To find an au pair, you generally go through an agency.

MISS POPPY'S GUIDE TO HAVING FUN

This age is a time of great change for your child. They may be starting school; perhaps they are dealing with the arrival of a new sibling. The world is unfolding before them, and it is important that you counteract the pressures and difficulties that this will involve with a good, healthy dose of what childhood should be all about: fun.

Here are a few ideas to help you keep playtime amusing, diverting and educational for your little one. It is the best gift you can give them.

MISS POPPY'S TOP BOOKS FOR THE OLDER TODDLER
Madeline, BY LUDWIG BEMELMANS
The Little Engine That Could, BY WATTY PIPER
The Little Red Hen, BY PAUL GALDONE
Goodnight Moon, BY MARGARET WISE BROWN

Green Eggs and Ham, BY DR SEUSS
If You Give a Mouse a Cookie, BY LAURA JOFFE NUMEROFF
Where The Wild Things Are, BY MAURICE SENDAK
The Curious George stories, BY MARGRET REY
Make Way For Ducklings, BY ROBERT MCCLOSKEY
What Mummies Do Best/What Daddies Do Best,
BY LAURA JOFFE NUMEROFF

MISS POPPY'S TOP TOYS FOR THE OLDER TODDLER

Wooden alphabet and number puzzles

Cotton reels

Animal and number snap cards

A pop-up tunnel for crawling through

Large lego bricks

A play kitchen complete with fake food, saucepans and

Cleaning utensils

Dressing-up clothes

Play dough

Musical toys: tambourines, drums, triangles, xylophones, sleigh bells

A toy farm set

A tub of plastic animals, dinosaurs, insects or reptiles

MISS POPPY'S DRESSING-UP TIPS

Dressing up is a fantastic way of engaging a child's creativity, and even of preventing the dreaded tantrum. My experience has taught me that many tantrums occur because a child is unable to express themselves and they just lose control. In these cases I have noticed an improvement if the child is allowed to play fantasy games and dress up. It is a creative outlet for them, and they seem to gain understanding, power and confidence by becoming a knight in shining armour, a superhero, a firefighter, a police officer, a mother, a father or a teacher. Gathering together bits and bobs for a dressing-up trunk does not have to be an expensive ordeal, the more the child has to use their imagination, the better. Wander around the house and see what you can find: an old pair of gloves, Daddy's old suit, shirt or tie, old hats and scarves, handbags, dresses, shawls and high heels. Bandages, plasters and empty medicine or vitamin bottles make for an excellent hospital room. Charity shops and flea markets are good sources of second-hand dressing-up props. Plastic swords and police and firefighter helmets can be found quite cheaply at toy shops. Use your imagination: a pair of angel or butterfly wings can be made easily with two pieces of cut-out card (construction paper) wildly decorated and attached with a piece of elastic to their arms. Keep dressing-up clothes and props in an old trunk or suitcase, or devote a drawer, basket or even a decorated cardboard box to keeping them together.

MISS POPPY'S TOP TODDLER GAMES

OBSTACLE COURSE

All my charges have loved this game which can be played inside or outside. With the help of your child, gather up cushions or pillows, laundry baskets, empty cardboard boxes, a waste-paper bin, a broom and a couple of chairs, and begin to build an obstacle course. Pillows or cushions make for a good set of stepping stones, a broom handle placed over two chairs is fun to crawl under or jump over. Laundry baskets or cardboard boxes are great for jumping into. Waste-paper baskets are ideal for having to aim and throw a ball into before you can continue along the course. For a bit of added extra fun, time with a stopwatch how long it takes to complete the course. They will love to try and beat their record time. And don't forget to tidy up together afterwards, happy and exhausted.

ANIMAL NOISES

Draw on small pieces of plain paper different animals, say a cow, a dog, a sheep, a pig and a lion. Fold them up and place them all mixed together in a hat or a bowl and let the children choose one each. They then have to make the noise of their animal.

HIDE THE PENNY

Simply hide a bunch of pennies all over the house or garden and let your little ones loose to find them.

MISS POPPY'S ARTS AND CRAFTS

SELF PORTRAITS

You will need:

> A large sheet of plain card (construction paper) the size of your child
> Poster paints
> Wool or string
> Old material or old clothes
> Buttons, coloured paper, tissue paper, cotton-wool balls – whatever bits and bobs you can find
> A pencil
> Scissors
> Glue
> A paintbrush

Ask your child to lie down on the plain piece of card, leaving room for you to trace around them. Once you have drawn their outline, they can get to work recreating themselves. Old clothes can be cut up to create an outfit; wool and string or cotton-wool balls can be painted to match their hair colour. The results are generally quite intriguing!

When they have finished, hang the figure up on the wall or the back of the door at ground level so your child can measure their growth against it.

HOME-MADE BOOKS

You will need:

> Plain or coloured paper (construction paper)
> Plain or coloured card
> Crayons, felt tips or coloured pencils
> Poster paints
> A stapler

Children love to admire and discuss their very own handiwork, and what a better way to enhance their creativity than by making a book out of all their drawings? Begin by painting or drawing a picture to start the story, or they may have a painting they have already done that they wish to begin with. On a separate piece of paper, write down in a few words what your child tells you about the picture. They may let you write at the bottom of the picture, but some children get upset by this. Continue the story with more pictures and ask your child to explain what is happening so that you can write it down. Once they tell you the story is complete, make a book cover by folding a piece of card in two and stapling the pictures and text inside. Let your child design the cover. Voila! Their first novel.

As we bid our fond farewell, my hope is that *Miss Poppy's Guide to Raising Perfectly Happy Children* has been rather like a visit from a first-class nanny – without the inconvenience of having to remortgage your house to provide a nanny flat, a car, spa visits, Gucci handbags and gym membership! I hope that it has helped by gently guiding you along the way to raising and producing happy, contented, inquisitive, kind and well-mannered children. I hope I will have convinced you that the most important factor for a growing child is fun! By sprinkling an inkling of fun you are more likely to get a response and gain cooperation and immediate attention, all of which lead to good learning skills and, most of all, happy memories of childhood – and at the end of the day, that, in my book, is what it's all about.

Remember that there is no perfect way to parent: you learn as you go along by trusting yourself and your instincts. There are so many things you have to do as a parent: be fair, be firm, be fun, be calm, be engaging, be responsive, beware … but most of all be there. And don't let it pass you by – a wise woman once told me childhood is a short season…

index

AUTHOR'S ACKNOWLEDGEMENTS

I dedicate this book to Alonzo Church Addison - my everything.
For your loving kindness, constant support and your never-ending intelligent curiosity - I thank you.

Thank you to: Rose, Tatiana, Jack and their practically perfect parents in every way - for the happiest of times; Denise Bates - a quiet hero - for her tasteful vision and intelligent insight; the fabulous Bailey sisters - Sarah Bailey for her magnificent management skills and Joanna Bailey for truly being the bestest friend a girl could ever have. And to all the wonderful parents and their individually charismatic children whom I had had the greatest pleasure in getting to know over the years.

Excerpts from: *Lady Bird: A Biography of Mrs. Johnson*, Jan Jarboe Russell, Rowman & Littlefield Publishing Group, Maryland, USA; *To Dance with God*, Gertrud Mueller Nelson, Copyright © 1986 by Gertrud Mueller Nelson, Paulist Press Inc., New York/Mahwah, N.J. Used with permission of Paulist Press. www.paulistpress.com; *Now We Are Six*, A.A. Milne, Heinemann Young Books, Harcourt Inc, Orlando, USA; *A Light in the Attic*, Shel Silverstein, Marion Boyars Publishers London, UK.

All reasonable efforts have been made by the Publishers to contact copyright holders. However, in the event of an omission or query please contact the Publishers who will be pleased to rectify the position.